INVISIBLE VICTIMS:
HOMELESSNESS AND THE GROWING SECURITY GAP

Despite Western society's preoccupation with safety and protection, its most vulnerable members still lack access to the level of security that many of us take for granted. In this trailblazing study, Laura Huey illustrates the issue of a 'security gap' faced by increasing homeless populations: while they are among the most likely victims of crime, they are also among the least served by existing forms of state and private security.

Invisible Victims presents the first comprehensive, integrated study of the risks faced by homeless people and their attempts to find safety and security in often dangerous environments. Huey draws not only on current debates on security within criminology, but also on a decade's worth of her own field research on the victimization and policing of the homeless. A theoretically and empirically informed examination of the myriad issues affecting the homeless, *Invisible Victims* makes a compelling case for society to provide necessary services and, above all, a basic level of security for this population.

LAURA HUEY is an associate professor in the Department of Sociology at the University of Western Ontario.

LAURA HUEY

Invisible Victims

Homelessness and the Growing Security Gap

UNIVERSITY OF TORONTO PRESS
Toronto Buffalo London

ISBN 978-1-4426-4328-4 (cloth)
ISBN 978-1-4426-1176-4 (paper)

Printed on acid-free, 100% post-consumer recycled paper with vegetable-based inks.

Library and Archives Canada Cataloguing in Publication

Huey, Laura
Invisible victims: homelessness and the growing security gap / Laura Huey.

Includes bibliographical references and index.
ISBN 978-1-4426-4328-4 (bound). ISBN 978-1-4426-1176-4 (pbk.)

1. Homeless persons – Social conditions. 2. Homeless persons – Crimes
against. I. Title.

HV4493.H83 2012   305.5'692   C2012-900758-7

This book has been published with the help of a grant from the J.B. Smallman
Publication Fund and the Faculty of Social Science, The University of Western
Ontario.

University of Toronto Press acknowledges the financial assistance to its publishing
program of the Canada Council for the Arts and the Ontario Arts Council.

Canada Council   Conseil des Arts
for the Arts   du Canada

ONTARIO ARTS COUNCIL
CONSEIL DES ARTS DE L'ONTARIO

University of Toronto Press acknowledges the financial support for its publishing
activities of the Government of Canada through the Canada Book Fund.

For R.V.E. – thank you

Contents

Illustrations

Acknowledgments

Putting together a manuscript requires a great deal of support and this book was no exception. First, I would like to offer my sincerest thanks to my friend, Junior, for allowing me to use his artwork for the cover of this book: I could not think of a more beautiful or appropriate image (the original piece can be seen at www.fdgrafx.com). I also owe a debt of gratitude to Marianne Quirouette, whose collaboration with me over the past few years has not only been satisfyingly productive but immensely enjoyable as well. One could not ask for a better comrade to be with in the trenches. I have also benefited from working with Eric Berndt, who has been forced to deal with some of the unusual situations I find myself in the field and has, like Marianne, done so with grace and good humour. I would also like to thank Doug Hildebrand and the editorial team at UTP. Doug's shepherding of this project made it both possible and significantly less stressful. One of the articles that I cite from in this book was co-authored by Tom Kemple, who spent many afternoons helping me work through my ideas when I was a doctoral student. I haven't forgotten your generosity, Tom. Ryan Broll, Danielle Hyrniewicz, and Georgios Fthenos were research assistants on the 2008 project. Thank you guys, and sorry that I ask such long-winded questions! My number one editor is my husband, Peter Halpern. Peter, thank you for reading my work and for just laughing when I start screaming about why one word is more useful than another.

INVISIBLE VICTIMS:
HOMELESSNESS AND THE GROWING SECURITY GAP

Introduction

We followed the nurse through the dimly lit corridor. When she reached the door, she knocked and pushed it open. After we ensured that the occupant was awake, introductions were made and the nurse left. Our new acquaintance smiled, patted her bed, and invited us to come in and sit down. I grabbed a chair, a nervous looking Eric perched uncomfortably on the woman's bed.

It was 2007 and my graduate student, Eric Berndt, and I were in a hospice that treats homeless patients. We had come to interview a woman who was a long-time survivor of homelessness, having spent many years living on the streets of Ottawa. Our goal was to try to understand some of the strategies that homeless women employ in order to stay safe on the streets and in the shelters (Huey and Berndt 2008). Although the woman we interviewed was bright and funny that day, regaling us with stories of having survived domestic abuse, violence on the streets, and a number of other forms of victimization, she was clearly dying. Later, as Eric and I shared our notes on the interview, I could not help but reflect on the fact that she was fortunate to be in the hospice. Had she still been out on the streets, unable to protect herself, she would have either had to rely on others to keep her safe or been preyed upon. I knew this from observation elsewhere.

My first real awareness of how utterly vicious life on the streets can be for homeless citizens came courtesy of an interview I did in Edinburgh in 2003 with two elderly street drinkers (Huey 2007). Long-time friends, they sat down together to discuss their experiences of how the area they inhabited – the Cowgate – was being policed. After a few moments, I noticed that one fellow was doing all of the talking and that the other man was often inarticulate. As they responded to questions as to whether they would ever report theft or other forms of victimization to the police, I began to get a better sense of the nature of their relationship. The chatty fellow had assumed the role of a protector when he discovered that his friend – in his sixties and terminally ill – was being repeatedly robbed by younger men at a local shelter. 'I try to look after him. Cancer,' he explained. 'I think people at the [shelter] take his money from him. Now, he's no' losing as much as he was losing' (ibid.: 44). None of the robberies were ever reported to police.

Life on the streets is hard, and many of those who find themselves homeless early in life will die young through disease, addiction, and the effects of chronic stress and malnutrition (Roy, Haley, Leclere, Sochanski, Boudreau, and Boivin 2004; Cheung and Hwang 2004; Hwang 2000; Boivin, Haley, and Lemire 1998). During their time on the streets, most will be victimized both economically and physically, and most will experience multiple victimizations (D'Ercole and Struening 1990; Wenzel et al. 2001; Evans and Forsyth 2004; Weseley and Wright 2009). The majority of these experiences will remain unreported to police and other authorities, and the physical and mental effects of sexual and violent victimization will go largely untreated (Huey and Quirouette 2009, 2010; Jasinski et al. 2005, 2010; Stermac and Paradis 2001). For far too many homeless citizens, criminal victimization is just another part of their lived reality, a fact of life that has to be endured, if not always accepted.

Homeless citizens are invisible victims (Wardhaugh 2000). Their stories are seldom captured within the 'official' crime-rate statistics poured over by criminologists, there are no milk cartons bearing their faces, and actors do not portray the stories of their victimization in vignettes for Crime Stoppers. They are 'hidden victims of crime with a frequency which would not be tolerated amongst the wider population' (Ballintyne 1999: 74). The irony of this invisibility is that it is occurring at a time when victims' rights groups and their criminal-justice agendas have been achieving greater recognition among policy makers. Homeless victims do not benefit from such initiatives because their voices are not heard; and, even if they were heard, their views would likely be discounted on the ground that they are 'undeserving victims,' individuals whose misfortunes are of their own making. Besides, as bearers of a suspect status, they are more easily cast as the target of public measures ostensibly enacted to promote public safety.

Those citizens who are dissatisfied with the measure of security they are provided within the public sphere have an easy remedy: with sufficient funds, they can simply seek solutions from the private-security sector. Here, too, homeless citizens are excluded. As 'failed consumers' (Bauman 2007), they lack the means to enter this market and purchase its products and services.

The Argument

Writing in 1992, sociologist David Lyon surveyed the impact of an inter-related set of technological, economic, and social changes that he saw as fundamentally altering the liberal-democratic landscape: 'The threat of a maximum security society emerging,' he warned, 'is a reality' (1992: 159). Lyon was writing of the potential for networked systems of data capture and collation to be used as surveillance tools in shadowing in-dividuals and populations; however, his comments about the rise of a 'maximum- security society' were borne out in ways far beyond Lyons's more limited focus on surveillance. Over the past few decades, we have witnessed in the West an incredible growth in demand for security measures. And yet, as I briefly alluded to above, while many of us are significantly more secure than our ancestors ever were, there remain segments of our populations who, in the great push for increasing security, have clearly been left behind.

What does it mean to live an insecure life in what is increasingly becoming a maximum-security society? To look around and see grow-ing numbers of private-security personnel and CCTV cameras and to know that they are not there to protect you? To sleep in an alley at night and be keenly aware of the fact that, if a police officer sees you, his or her primary concern will likely not be your safety but to move you along so that your presence doesn't offend or invoke fear in others? To live with the knowledge that you are very likely going to have your things stolen or destroyed, be harassed and threatened and physically or sexu-ally assaulted, but have few options to address your own very real fears? And, when the inevitable victimization happens, that your pain and suffering will likely remain completely invisible?

In the pages that follow, I draw on data from research conducted with homeless victims of crime to flesh out the extent to which this group of citizens lives insecure lives. The existence of the security gap that home-less citizens face tells us much about the relative state of citizenship within contemporary liberal democracies. As the foundation stone of the 'original bargain' between citizen and state, security represents not only a subjective, ideal state of being but a public good that all citizens are entitled to as a right of citizenship. Thus, the fact of unequal provisioning and access to security among populations – that is, the existence of security gaps – is indicative of not only the stratified nature of society but the stratified nature of citizenship and civil rights. In essence, then, the main premise of this book is that the security gap that homeless men, women, and children experience denotes, in very tangible ways, their status as 'lesser citizens' (Rose 1999) and that true equality for the homeless citizen necessarily entails the equalization of security through forms of redistribution.

Sources[1]

In order to explore the nature and meaning of the security gaps identified, I draw on data collected from my own research over the past ten years on victimization and the policing of homeless populations.[2] This data is derived from three different studies.[3]

The first of these studies is my own doctoral dissertation research: a comparative project on the policing of urban areas commonly referred to as 'skid row' districts. From 2000 to 2003, I examined the policing of 'skid rows' in Vancouver, Edinburgh, and San Francisco in order to explore how urban political economies shape the style of policing employed 'on the margins.' For this study, I engaged in ethnographic fieldwork in each city and conducted one hundred and one (n=101) semi-structured interviews with police, homeless citizens, homelessness-service providers, civic officials, local business people, and other area residents. The results were subsequently published in 2007 as *Negotiating Demands: The Politics of Skid Row Policing in Edinburgh, San Francisco, and Vancouver.* As is often the case, though, I collected far more material than I was able to immediately use, and some of this data were subsequently published in journal articles (Huey and Berndt 2008; Huey 2009).

During the course of interviewing homeless women for the 2003 study, I became aware of the fact that some women utilize gender-based survival strategies as a means of increasing their safety on the streets. In 2007 I decided to explore this phenomenon further and so returned to the field with Eric Berndt. We conducted twenty-five (n=25) in-depth qualitative interviews with homeless women and community-service providers in Montreal and Ottawa. Participants were asked a series of questions that focused on security-related issues facing women on the streets; personal experiences of criminal victimization; crime fears and feelings of vulnerability; security strategies for responding to potential threats of victimization; and presentations of gender. Some of the data from this study were published in 2008 (Huey and Berndt 2008).

The third study I draw from examined the willingness of stakeholders in two Canadian cities to consider using third-party reporting to facilitate homeless victims' access to policing services based on a program developed in Edinburgh. One hundred and thirteen interviews (n=113) were conducted during three phases of research. The first phase involved returning to Edinburgh with Marianne Quirouette to evaluate the operation of the model program. While there, we interviewed police, service organizations, and homeless-service users about issues related to crime, victimization, security, and access to justice. We then returned to Canada to begin work in the two cities selected: Toronto and Vancouver. In both cities, we used similar questions to those posed in Edinburgh in interviews with police, service providers, and homeless citizens. The final result was a technical report making several key recommendations for improving policing services for homeless victims of crime (Huey and Quirouette 2008), as well as a couple of related articles (Huey 2010; Huey and Quirouette 2010).

A Blueprint

I have tried to organize this book in a way that will make it accessible to the widest audience possible. To that end, the first chapter serves as a gentle introduction to some of the relevant literature on security and the increased demand for this public good across Western polities. The primary focus of this chapter is, however, not 'the state of security' but rather the centrality of security as a 'public good' in both traditional and contemporary modes of understanding what it means to be a citizen within liberal democracies. This discussion is thus intended to provide a context for understanding the full implications of the security gap that homeless citizens face in relation to understanding their place in society.

In order to give readers a sense of the dimensions of this gap, chapters 2 through 5 flesh out a number of important issues related to victimization, to the homeless citizen's pursuit of security, and to the limitations of their available security options. Chapter 2 begins this examination with a thorough discussion of various forms of criminal victimization experienced by homeless citizens, from petty theft to murder. Since increased risk of victimization is linked to a number of key social factors, particular attention is paid to those groups that are uniquely vulnerable: women, youth, the elderly, the mentally ill, and queer and/or transgendered citizens.

To the extent that security is linked to citizenship and the state maintains its role as the primary provider of this public good, it is important to understand how state-based forms of security are provided to homeless citizens and the inherent limitations of those forms. In Chapter 3 I examine public police services and how various factors inhibit the willingness of homeless citizens to report crimes to police. In some instances, reasons provided for failures to report by homeless citizens mirror those found in surveys of the general public. However, there are also other factors present that are unique to homeless and other street-based populations. First, there is the often complex nature of the relationship between homeless citizens and the police. Whereas some homeless individuals view the police as legitimate authorities with the ability to provide even-handed security in an often difficult world, still others – indeed, frequently a majority – see the police as antagonistic and not to be trusted. Trust also plays a role in relation to the second factor identified. To the extent that homelessness remains a stigmatized social status, this status operates as a barrier to reporting by undermining the individual's confidence that their reports will be believed and responded to seriously, and/or that they themselves will not become suspect. The third factor that limits the willingness of homeless citizens to report victimization to police is the existence of a 'snitching code' which operates within the local subculture. Homeless victims frequently must successfully negotiate this code or risk further peril by being branded a 'rat' or 'grass.'

Given the limits of state-based forms of security and the inability of the homeless citizen to access private-security forms available to the consumer classes, homeless citizens must develop their own strategies to stay safe within spaces that render them vulnerable to increased risk of victimization. The focus of chapter 4 is the individual tactics that homeless citizens employ as means of trying to fill the security gap they face. A range of such strategies are identified: the cultivation of 'street smarts,' the development of a tough persona, avoidance and target-hardening tactics, and the use of violence to address threats to physical security.

While developing individual survival skills is necessary to securing one's safety on the streets, the reality is that most homeless citizens form ties to each other and their community, ties that can assist them in staying safe. Thus, the focus of chapter 5 is on how homeless citizens seek and access security through relationships with others. For example, intimate partners play a critical role in enhancing individual security, as do friends and acquaintances. As well, to the extent that community-service organizations have a stake in ensuring the continued use of their facilities, the provision of various forms of security to patrons has become a routine function of their work. The ways in which shelters, day centres, and other facilities – and those who work within a service capacity – attempt to provide security for clients are considered.

Whereas previous chapters focus on issues related to victimization and security strategies, in chapter 6 I examine the issue of what security and the security gap means to homeless citizens. Drawing on interview data, I demonstrate that security does matter to many homeless citizens, particularly when the costs of victimization are tallied. To that end, I also examine the fact that, as invisible victims of crimes, this group frequently bears significant physical and mental costs associated with their victimization and the insecurity it breeds. Chief among these costs is the knowledge that their relative state of insecurity denotes a status of 'lesser citizen,' marking them as individuals unworthy of the protections of the larger society.

In chapter 7 I return to the contention discussed in chapter 1 that security is something of which individuals, groups, and societies can have too much (Zedner 2003). What I suggest is that security in and of itself is not problematic; rather, the issue lies in its uneven distribution. I thus argue for a redistribution of security, and do so by suggesting various ways in which such redistribution could easily begin to be achieved.

1 Security and Citizenship

A: I think there is a lot of wrong being done out there. If you can lessen that, I'm all for it, even if that means a couple extra [CCTV] cameras.
Q: So, in your mind, if it's going to enhance security, then it's cool?
A: Yeah, security and protecting people.

– Homeless male, Vancouver

It's not unusual for people to ask whether I'm ever concerned for my own safety when I'm working on the streets. The answer is usually no. As a non-resident of the areas I work in, my risk of victimization is usually minimal. Nobody on the streets wants to have the police bearing down on them or their community because a middle-class, middle-aged, white female professor was robbed. It also helps that over the years I have learned to avoid potentially risky situations. This was not always the case.

My learning process began in 2003 when, flush with the freedom that comes with being a PhD student turned loose, I began fieldwork in the Cowgate district of Edinburgh. Having previously worked in Vancouver's Downtown Eastside (DTES), I thought I was sufficiently street-wise and thus prepared for anything. On my second day in Edinburgh, I realized otherwise. I had decided to introduce myself to some of the community-service organizations that dot the Cowgate. One of the places on my list, a medical clinic serving the area's homeless, was difficult to locate. I saw what appeared to be a street entrance, but the door was locked and nobody answered my knocking. A few hours later, I went back and found a young woman sitting on the building's steps. I explained my confusion to her and she replied that she was a client of the clinic, waiting to see a doctor. Apparently, the entrance to the clinic was not in the front of the building, but down a narrow close[1] along the side. Stating that the entrance might not be easy for a stranger to find, she got up to show me. I quickly found myself walking through a narrow, covered close with a complete stranger behind me. In the darkness of the close, I became acutely aware of exactly how vulnerable I was. If she had decided to rob me, I would have been fairly defenceless. Mere seconds later, I was at the clinic door, relief flooding through me as I realized that the woman was nothing more than a Good Samaritan. In those few seconds, security was not some elusive, intangible abstraction but a very real and desirable state.

In this chapter, I present a brief look at some of the concepts that are central to the core of ideas contained within this book. In looking at security, citizenship, and important issues linked to both, I hope to provide a meaningful context for the material that follows.

Security

We all need some kind of law and order. We need to know that there is a safety net and that it is gonna help us and support us.
– Service provider, Edinburgh

As with other abstract concepts, nailing down a concrete definition of security can be a rather tricky task. Within this book I use the term security to denote a *relative* state of physical and ontological freedom from both immediate and potential criminal threats. In using the bracketing term 'criminal threats,' this definition includes two key components: physical safety (crimes against the person), and the safety of one's personal belongings (crimes against property[2]). The inclusion of a future-oriented component to conceptualizing security is, I feel, also an important element. In order to have a sense of ontological security, or a sense of inner peace as some scholars prefer to term it, one must be reasonably free from the burden of constant wariness and anxiety over future threat.[3]

Why is physical and ontological peace viewed as desirable? At the level of the individual, security can be understood as a state of being that affords one the ability to pursue his/her own self-interest. Freed from having to continuously manage threats within their environment, citizens are able to seek out means of fulfilling their aspirations (Ericson 2007). At the level of the collective, security provides the conditions – the stability, the trust – necessary for various forms of social, economic, and other exchange. Borrowing from I. Loader and N. Walker (2007: 8), we could say that security is a 'thick' public good that is fundamental to the task of holding polities together: 'Security, in other words, is simultaneously the producer and product of forms of trust and abstract solidarity between intimates and strangers that are prerequisite to democratic political communities.'

In his analysis of the origins of the liberal state, Michel Foucault (1997) argues that the primary public good sought through this particular form of governance is that of maximized economies.[4] Among the conditions necessary for the growth of such economies is internal and external security, since enterprise requires orderly relations among individuals and groups. Understood this way, security is not simply a benefit of citizenship, it is simultaneously a state of being, a set of processes and a goal that is the very raison d'être of the liberal-democratic state (ibid.).

Earlier scholars shared this view of security as the glue that binds individuals and communities together. Perhaps the most well-known argument for this position is found in Thomas Hobbes's *Leviathan* (1985 [1651]). Looking to 'human nature' as the cause of continual strife, Hobbes argued that what humans require is a strong centralized power to counterbalance the lure of violence as a tool for making individuals 'masters of other men's persons, wives, children and cattle' or for using violence to protect their own (ibid.: 185). Without 'a common power to keep them all in awe,' he suggested, humans will pursue self-interest at any cost and thus remain in a continual state of war (ibid.: 204). To create peaceable conditions requires common agreement to unite under the rule of a government, the task of which is to enforce peace, both within and outside the boundaries of the state. Thus, for Hobbes, the purpose and goal of liberal citizenship is to 'provide insecure citizens with protection within a secure state and insecure states with protection from their citizens. Leviathan, then, is the original modern liberal design for safe living based upon a specific imagining of the citizen/violence relationship in a sovereign society. As such, Leviathan links citizenship not only with design; it links citizenship with protection ... what all this means, then, is that it is actually more difficult to separate citizenship from safety and design than it is to think these ideas together' (Weber 2008: 130).

Such views of the nature of liberal citizenship were notably shared by Jean-Jacques Rousseau (1939 [1762]: 32), who argued that individuals who agreed to live together in collective forms 'made an advantageous exchange: instead of an uncertain and precarious way of living they have got one that is better and more secure; instead of natural independence they have got liberty, instead of the power to harm others security for themselves, and instead of their strength, which others might overcome, a right which social union makes invincible.'

Citizenship

I think most [homeless] people sort of feel, at the very least, really disconnected from mainstream society.

– Service provider, Vancouver

Who is this citizen who trades for the constraints and freedoms to be found within collective security? Traditionally, citizenship has been narrowly defined as a legal status derived from membership in a political community (Rubenstein 2000). However, as with security, citizenship has been a frequently contested concept. It is also one that has proven to be highly mutable, its meanings and attendant rights evolving over time. Among social changes that have influenced this evolution were the rise of Keynesianism and the creation of the welfare state in the first half of the twentieth century. Adoption of the Keynesian view that it is the responsibility of the state to ameliorate the social conditions produced by the vagaries of a free market led to a recasting of the roles of both the state and the citizen. It also opened the door to subsequent reworkings of this concept by scholars seeking a means of denoting citizenship as encompassing normative concepts such as social inclusion and substantive equality. Of these analyses, likely none has been more influential than the work of T.H. Marshall (1950).

For Marshall (1996), citizenship in liberal democracies is composed of three sets of civil, political, and social rights. Civil rights are those individual freedoms commonly associated with liberal regimes, such as the right to own property, freedom of religion, freedom of speech, and so on; political rights permit the participation of citizens in the exercise of political power through free elections, balloting rights, and the like. Where Marshall deviates from earlier notions of citizenship is in his articulation of the existence of social rights, a series of prescriptions aimed at ameliorating some of the inequities produced within capitalist systems. This cluster of rights he characterizes as including a 'modicum of economic welfare and security to the right to share to the full in the social heritage and to live the life of a civilized being according to the standards prevailing in the society' (ibid.: 149). Such inclusionary visions were to predominate in public policy and discourse across the West for the next couple of decades. However, ultimately, what some have termed the 'golden age of welfarism' proved to be short-lived (Young 1999). In the wake of its demise, what was revealed was the full extent to which social rights proved to be anything but inalienable.[5]

What led to the undoing of the Marshallian vision of inclusionary social citizenship was the adoption of a public-policy course intended to create a number of deep structural changes. The trigger for this shift was the economic crisis of the 1970s. Confronted with growing inflation and a significant oil crisis, policy makers first, then their publics, began not only to question current economic policies but also to cast a sceptical eye on issues of social rights, particularly the desirability of public spending on state-based economic-redistribution schemes. Politicians were aided in the development of their positions on these matters by a number of influential advisers wholly convinced of the rightness of the tenets of the American variant of neo-liberalism. This model of neo-liberalism was adopted widely in the United States and to a lesser extent in Britain and other countries (O'Malley 2004; Huey 2009).

Most significantly, in those countries that adopted the American neo-liberal model wholly or in significant pieces, the introduction of this form of political economy led to a radical reworking of the relationship between the economic and social spheres of governance. No longer seen as a desirable means of improving the conditions of those disadvantaged within the market economy, social-welfare programs run by an 'inefficient state' were recast as harmful to society. In the eyes of conservative commentators, the welfare state was responsible not only for the creation of a culture of dependency among the poor (Fraser and Gordon 1989) but for every social ill imaginable – from teenage pregnancies to the 'crack' epidemic of the 1980s (Gilder 1981; Murray 1984, 1999; Marsland 1996). Although acknowledging the social and economic factors that structure aid recipients' situations, even liberal commentators were not averse to pointing out what they deemed to be blameworthy individual and cultural causes of 'dependency' (Wilson 1987; Ellwood 1988; Jencks 1992). In a cultural climate now hostile to the idea of 'handouts,' a host of old and new pathological images – from 'welfare queens' to 'bag ladies' – were trotted out to be eagerly consumed by an increasingly fearful and angry public. As Zygmunt Bauman (2007: 31) suggests, in the public imaginary, aid recipients, indeed the non-working poor more generally, became 'the yarn from which nightmares are woven –

though as the official version would rather have it, they are ugly yet greedy weeds, which add nothing to the harmonious beauty of the garden but famish the plants, sucking out and devouring a lot of the feed.' Where possible and practicable, the task of governments became to reform 'social leeches,' turning them instead into honest, productive workers. This goal would be met either through punitive public-policy measures or, where practicable, by turning to the private sector for solutions. To assist the reform process, the social-safety net was increasingly shrunk through the implementation of restrictive accessibility requirements, benefit term limits, and policies aimed at pushing people off the public-welfare roll.

Previously I have argued that political economies are 'moral economies' in that they reflect the underlying values of a given culture (Huey 2007). The American variant of neo-liberalism is based on a meritocratic ideal that privileges autonomy, enterprise, risk taking, skill, and prudence (Ericson, Barry, and Doyle 2000). Under previous conceptions of citizenship, the citizen was seen as a passive rights bearer to whom obligations were owed by the state. In those Western nations that adopted elements of American neo-liberalism – or what Nikolas Rose (1999) has termed 'advanced liberal' societies – discussion of duties and obligations gave way, in whole or in part, to a new market-based ethos within which the citizen became an active consumer of both public and private services. As Rose explains, 'the active citizen was one who was an entrepreneur of him- or herself. This was not simply a re-activation of values of self-reliance, autonomy and independence as the underpinning of self-respect, self-esteem, self-worth and self-advancement. It is rather that the individual was to conduct his or her life, and that of his or her family, as a kind of enterprise, seeking to enhance and capitalize on existence itself through calculated acts and investments' (ibid.: 164).

The restructuring of the relationship of the individual to the state is said to have done more than recast our notion of what constitutes the citizen; it also sounded the death knell of universalistic ideals of citizenship, those romantic imaginings in which all individuals by virtue of birth would automatically possess common social, political, and economic rights and entitlements guaranteed by the state. Additionally, this restructuring has purportedly left us with a very exclusive definition of citizenship: one in which rights are directly linked to the exercise of civic responsibilities, foremost of which is to function as productive producers and consumers within the marketplace (Young 1999; Rose 1999; Bauman 2007).

Nostalgic glimpses backward to an imagined past often fail to account for a central fact about citizenship and rights discourse: both have always been inherently exclusionary (Turner 2009). Indeed, the very status of 'citizen' entails not only membership and community for some but lack of membership for others (Sklar 1991). We see the same thing in relation to rights discourse. The notion that civil or human rights are inalienable is a piece of romantic Enlightenment fiction. As Hannah Arendt (2000 [1951]) amply demonstrates in her analysis of the Declaration of the Rights of Man, the successful invocation of a right requires the existence of both a state guarantee and a recognized claim to citizenship. Certainly, the experience of Jewish citizens in Germany in the early part of the twentieth century illustrates how quickly individuals and groups can be dispossessed of legal, political, and social rights. And, as Arendt suggests, the case of the European Jews is not exceptional in this regard: there are any number of ethnic, religious, or other groups who currently exist as 'rightless people.'

Not only are there absolute cases of non-citizens lacking rights, but within economically and socially stratified societies there exist individuals who, by virtue of birth, have the legal status of citizen but enjoy access to few of the rights and benefits of citizenship. Such situations occur because citizenship itself is a stratified concept, and individuals therefore enjoy different degrees of citizenship and variable access to the rights to be bestowed upon citizens. And, because there is a significant degree of overlap between what constitutes 'society' and 'nation' or 'society' and the 'state,' stratified forms of citizenship are matched by degrees of social inclusion. This linkage and its social consequences have also been noted by Ruth Lister (1998: 7): 'Exclusion and inclusion operate at both a legal and sociological level through "formal" and "substantive" modes of citizenship. The former denotes the legal status of membership of a state, as symbolised by possession of a passport; the latter the enjoyment of the rights and obligations associated with membership and sometimes simply legal residence. At both the legal and sociological level, exclusion and inclusion represent a continuum rather than an absolute dichotomy. Thus, members of a society enjoy different degrees of substantive citizenship.'

Homeless individuals are easily numbered among those citizens who enjoy fewer political, social, and legal rights than other groups in civil society. Indeed, if we consider the ability to access rights and have them recognized by the state and polity as *the* mark of one's full citizenship, then we might, borrowing from Arendt (2000), see the homeless citizen as akin to a stateless person who happens to exist within the borders of a nation-state with little relation to it. While various commentators have provided ample justifications for this view of homeless citizens,[6] pointing to various civil and human rights routinely denied such people, my concern here is both more limited and, to my mind, more fundamental. If we strip away the various civil rights that have evolved to form modern notions of citizenship, we are left with a single, core purpose for the state and a single benefit of citizenship: security. If certain people are without security, or unable to access many, indeed most forms of security, are they citizens? And, if so, what kind of citizens are they?

The State of Security

People are disillusioned.
– Homeless male, Edinburgh, on the state's ability to protect all of its citizens

Of course, the questions posed above presuppose a view of security as not only a desirable public good but as the foundation upon which the edifice of liberal democracy is built. Some scholars would challenge these assumptions. Among them is Mark Neocleous (2008: 4), who believes that we ought to abandon the belief that security is a 'kind of universal or transcendental value,' instead of a tool for the exercise of power within capitalist modes of governance (see also Simon 2007). According to Neocleous, should we opt to rid ourselves of the view that security is a necessary condition for a successful or harmonious life, then we might begin to engage in a new emancipatory politics 'centred on a difference conception of the good' (ibid.: 186). In this radical reworking of the Hobbesian form of citizenship, we would simply learn to live with 'the insecurities that come from being human' (ibid.: 186). Presumably, according to this mode of thinking, living with violence, crime, and war is preferable to living in a maximum-security society.

Other analysts of contemporary security discourse, however, take a different tack: security remains a form of public good, just one that requires better governance (Johnston and Shearing 2003; Zedner 2003, 2009; Dupont 2006; Loader and Walker 2006). Security requires better governance because unchecked growth in this area, in both public and private domains, has exacerbated our exclusive tendencies, leading to a number of disastrous social consequences (Zedner 2003; 2009).

Certainly, over the past ten years or so, we have witnessed a staggering proliferation of public, private, and hybridized security forms, all of which are aimed at controlling crime and disorder (Stenson and Edwards 2001; Bauman 2006; Garland 2000). This growth, coupled with what appear to be ever-increasing demands for punitive public policies that will supposedly 'make us safer,' would seem to suggest that Western societies have developed a nearly insatiable appetite for security. Bauman (2006: 130) contends that what he terms our 'security obsession' is paradoxical on more than one level. First, he rightly notes that those who tend to be among the most insecure live in 'some of the most secure ... societies that ever existed' (ibid.: 129). In contrast to the millions of people who are currently living in battle zones, suffering through bloody civil wars, or being subjected to slavery and in other inhumane conditions, North Americans and Europeans tend to be a relatively pampered bunch. Second, Bauman reminds us that the constant search for ways of increasing security 'becomes the most prolific, self-replenishing and probably inexhaustible source of our anxiety and fear' (ibid.: 130).

It is obvious to even the most casual of observers that the modern desire for security – defined here as protection from criminal victimization – has a distinctly class-based foundation to it (Hope 2000; Young 2006; Ericson 2007; Crawford 2006; Bauman 2006). In particular, it is the middle classes – or, perhaps more accurately, the 'consumer classes' – who are seen to clamour for new laws to protect them from various threats while demanding more public police protection and consuming greater amounts of private forms of security (Hope 2000; Stenson 2001; Crawford 2006; Ericson 2007). Various explanations have been put forward to explain the rise in middle-class crime-related anxieties in several countries, ranging from the economic precariousness of life under the neo-liberal yoke (Young 1999, 2006; Simon 2001; Beckett and Herbert 2010) to the existential angst said to be produced by the risks attendant on increased plurality and weakened traditional social bonds (Giddens 1991; Garland 2001), or as part of a general cyclical trend (Tonry 2004). Whatever the cause, the mood of the consumer classes appears to be one of not only heightened insecurity but also of heightened intolerance towards any behaviour or being that suggests the remotest possibility of threat.

To be fair, the fact of heightened crime-related anxieties among members of the general public has not been helped by a number of social actors, who are seen to benefit directly from public fears. Among these groups is the mass media, which routinely exploits the sensational elements of even the most pedestrian of crimes in order to capture

'ratings share.' The state also plays an important role in the amplifica-
tion of fear through its various attempts at 'responsibilizing' citizens
into becoming active, educated managers of their own individual personal risks (O'Malley 1992; Garland 1996). The message that people
should look after their own security interests, coupled with the trim-
ming or withdrawal of various public crime-prevention and security-
related services, has had at least three significant net effects. The first is
a stoking of public anxieties, as the nation-state is seen to do less and
less for the public in the field of security. The second is that ambitious
politicians have seized opportunities to capture power through electoral
platforms that promise to placate fears through 'get tough on crime'
approaches (Simon 2007; Tonry 2004). Politicians now 'govern through
crime' (Simon 2007), because, as Nils Christie (2004: 37) explains, 'there
are so few other arenas left … for the national exposure of politicians as
political figures, and for the party line. Where the dominant goal of life
is money and the dominating idea is that an unregulated market economy is the road to this goal, in such a system crime becomes the major
area for what remains of politics. Here it is possible to present oneself
as a person deserving votes, with values common to a population of
affluent consumers.' The third result is that affluent consumers have
also begun to rely increasingly less on the state for security, turning
instead to private markets in their search for crime solutions (Loader
1999; Ericson 2006). In the consumer security market, we find yet another
cluster of actors who benefit from public fears, since anxious customers
mean more opportunities to sell or contract cameras, gates, alarms,
security guards, and so on (Loader 1999; Ericson and Haggerty 1997;
Haggerty 2003).

   If homeless citizens are not among those demanding increasing levels
of security or purchasing new gadgetry to outfit their non-existent
homes, then where does the homeless citizen fit within the new maximum-security society? The pursuit of security necessarily entails the
targeting and exclusion of groups identified as potential threats to public
safety and order (Zedner 2003). Not surprisingly, among identified
threats we find those groups that already exist on the fringes of society.
Being a heterogeneous population consisting of multiple figures of 'social
junk' (Spitzer 1975) – the mentally ill, the vagrant, the drunk, the unem-
ployable, the prostitute, and the pauper, among others – the homeless
represent a source of moral contamination and physical and economic
danger within the public imaginary (Parenti 1999; Rose 1999). Many
within the larger community believe that since homeless citizens 'are all

useless ... the society of consumers would gain if they vanished' (Bauman 2007: 32). To that end, the homeless citizen frequently becomes the target of public demands for exclusion-oriented legal and extra-legal practices aimed at erasing their visible presence from public space (Parenti 1999; Sullivan 2001; Arnold 2004; Huey 2007; Beckett and Herbert 2010). For the criminal justice system, and indeed many criminologists, the homeless citizen is a public risk that can no longer be rehabilitated but must instead be managed through actuarial, target-hardening, and other preventative and/or prophylactic measures (Garland 2001).

It is such exclusionary practices that cause Lucia Zedner (2003) to argue that, if security *is* a public good, then it is one of which we can have too much. Indeed, Zedner goes further and argues that the endless pursuit of this good can be 'inimical to the good society' because of its very real potential for social exclusion and other negative social effects that she enumerates (ibid.: 158). While this position is one with which I have much sympathy, it remains the case that the relationship of security and homeless citizenship is significantly more complex, as Zedner (2009) herself recognizes in her more recent work on the subject. This relationship thus requires a more thorough, nuanced analysis. If we simply dismiss security as a needless obsession of the affluent, seeing in it only the potential for increased exclusion of marginalized groups, we miss the fact that security as a public good is not problematic in and of itself, but rather that the problem lies in its distribution (see also Hope 2000; Zedner 2009). If some citizens have too much security, then others have not nearly enough.

The Security Gap

We're all street people. We live on the street. You got to look after yourself.
– Homeless male, Toronto

The distribution of a social or positional good is necessarily based on the ability of individual citizens and groups to access that good. And clearly, in order for some citizens to have too much of something and others not nearly enough, access has to be uneven or controlled in such a way as to limit or regulate its accessibility. But how does one go about accessing security or trying to create physical or ontological security in the first place? Obviously, the state is one such source, and the private security market another. A third is through private individual or collective efforts.

In his work on the development of modern governance, Foucault (1984; 1995 [1977]; 2003) traces the replacement of traditional forms of overt state regulation with sophisticated coordinate systems of micro-disciplinary techniques diffused throughout the social body. In analysing the historical development of 'policing' – employed in its broadest sense – Foucault (1984: 242) states: 'At any rate, it seems that, during the 18th and 19th centuries, there appear – rather quickly in the case of commerce and more slowly in all the other domains – this idea of a police that would manage to penetrate, to stimulate, to regulate, and to render almost automatic all the mechanisms of society.' Among those institutions that developed in order to 'be everywhere' and so attend to 'everything that happens' within a physical territory (Foucault 1977) are the public police. Their presence 'everywhere' is to serve the cause of social order through various repressive functions and through their ability to gather knowledge that is, in turn, fed back into the machinery of state.

Of course, the reality is that the public police cannot 'be everywhere.' However, the myth that through their presence they can stem the tide of crime has had an enduring appeal. So much so, in fact, that as the myth has been shown to be false over the past few decades, a number of scholars have charted a growing disenchantment with the police. This disenchantment, in turn, has presented the police institution with a number of significant challenges. Among those who have documented what they perceive to be a growing disillusionment with public policing as a social panacea is David Garland (1996, 2001). Writing in 1996, Garland contrasts the optimism of the 1950s and 1960s with the pessimism or cynicism found in present attitudes towards the state in general, and towards the criminal justice system in particular. In analysing this shift, Garland puts the matter succinctly: 'There is a new sense of the failure of criminal justice agencies and a more limited sense of the state's powers to regulate conduct and prohibit deviance' (1996: 47). This limited sense of the state's power to foster security through crime prevention or response is based on recognition of the fact that, ultimately, policing resources are finite. Tim Hope (2000: 98) advances a similar position, noting that police resources are a public good that is 'subject to crowding as a result of increased demand ... especially if police resources cannot be increased commensurately and yet are still to be offered on a universal basis' (see also Crawford 2006). This congestion, combined with what Garland terms the system's capacity limits, thus neatly rule out the possibility that the police can 'be everywhere.' Garland is of the view that 'this state of affairs is quite new, and has led to some significant developments. In particular, the perceived normality of high crime rates, together with the widely acknowledged limitations of criminal justice agencies, have begun to erode one of the foundational myths of modern societies: namely, the myth that the sovereign state is capable of providing security, law and order, and crime control within its territorial boundaries' (ibid.: 448).

In a previous book I argued that 'golden age' thinking on issues related to public welfare focus almost exclusively on how perceived social changes affect the middle classes, and fail to consider whether or how real or perceived impacts might affect those who inhabit the margins (Huey 2007). Despite growing fears and feelings of abandonment on the part of many who make up the middle classes, the effects of rationing of public forms of security are more easily absorbed by such groups. Where the attenuation of policing services is most keenly felt is among those who suffer disproportionately from higher crime rates and have fewer alternative resources to call upon. Logically, one would think that those with the highest demonstrable need for public police services would be the greater recipients of those services, even in times of increased demand and resource scarcity. But that is not what happens. As Richard Ericson (2007: 205) explains, when 'forced to make hard decisions and express authoritative certainty in doing so, law necessarily privileges one perspective on risk costs and benefits at the expense of others.' Because public police agencies rely directly on support from the public and the public purse, they must be seen to be attentive to the demands of vocal and/or powerful citizens. Not surprisingly, then, when the police decide on the distribution of their services, often the resulting cost-benefit calculations are tipped in favour of those citizens whose support is seen as necessary or desirable (Huey 2007). Such calculations clearly do not favour the homeless individual or other unprivileged citizens. As Ericson (2007: 205) also notes, the state, in the execution of its duties to its citizenry, wields a 'power that hurts, causes resentment, provokes a sense of injustice, produces insecurity, and poses again the problem of uncertainty.'

With the criminal justice system being seen by many citizens as inadequate or ineffective, the private security market – which has always been present as an alternative to state systems – has grown exponentially (Jones and Newburn, 1995; Garland 2001; Sanders, 2005). However, as I have already noted, this means of accessing security is largely closed off to the homeless citizen. Indeed, not only does the private market offer options unavailable to those without financial means, its security solutions often have serious negative impacts on marginalized citizens. Among these is the fact that its offerings are frequently arrayed against the homeless citizen and other urban poor, who have been constituted as suitable targets of crime-prevention efforts. Further, to the extent that the private security market remains largely unregulated, there are few, if any, mechanisms for public oversight and accountability (Rigakos 2002; Singh 2005). Thus, the homeless citizen who is harassed or abused by a private security guard often finds him or herself with few avenues for redress (Huey, Haggerty, and Ericson 2007). Another significant concern raised about the growth in commercial security provision is the fact that it is challenging the primacy of the state as *the* guarantor of security and fragmenting the provision of security (Loader 1999). This challenge is occurring as commercial organizations and the affluent come to prefer guaranteed access through the private market to rationed access through public policing (Garland 2001). That such consumers might seek to 'opt out' of paying or accessing public services altogether is a possibility with potentially deleterious effects. At present, the largest negative consequence of fragmentation is the creation of entrenched hierarchies of security access, wherein optimal access is based solely on socio-economic status, rather than individual need or some other criteria (Hope 2000). Zedner (2009: 89) worries that what is at stake is 'the enjoyment of security by all as a public good.' The consumer market in security also has negative displacement effects which have a disproportionate impact upon the lives of marginalized citizens (Zedner 2009). Crime is a social fact, a normal, everyday occurrence. Designing out crime through the built environment, implementing private security patrols, installing surveillance cameras within the walls of gated communities, none of these measures decrease the overall occurrence of crime. As Hope (2000: 88) explains, 'private security actions may also generate externality costs for others – that is, private-interest security actions may increase the risk of insecurity to others by producing "malign displacement" of risk in encouraging offenders to seek other, less-protected targets.' In effect, the private security sector consciously markets and facilitates the ultimate form of NIMBY-ism, in which unwanted individuals and activities become a burden that is shifted from the affluent onto the unprotected poor.

The third means of accessing security is through individual and collective efforts, with citizens becoming active self-managers of their individual security risks and/or participating together in efforts aimed at fostering security. While the language smacks of contemporary neo-liberal discourse, the reality is that homeless citizens have long been responsible for their individual and group security. This is not because the state has 'empowered' homeless communities through feel-good 'community-partnering' initiatives, but because it has more or less abdicated a significant portion of its responsibility for providing security to this class of citizens. This point was brought sharply into relief for me when I once asked a homeless man in San Francisco whether anyone in his community would report victimization to the police. His answer highlights the fact that, when the police or the larger society do acknowledge the existence of homeless victims, they tend to treat them as undeserving and therefore as unworthy of a police response. The police embody this viewpoint, he suggests, by letting 'the streets take care of themselves' (Huey and Kemple 2007: 2316). This is not to say that the state has completely abdicated its responsibilities, but what state security coverage does exist is minimal and, as I show in chapter 3, regarded with scepticism if not outright suspicion by individuals who are more used to being treated as suspects by state agents than as legitimate citizens. As a result of their sense of abandonment by the state, homeless citizens must devise strategies to look after their own safety and security. Certainly, in this regard they are not unique; however, what distinguishes the homeless citizen from other more affluent groups in society is the extent to which they have few viable alternative choices when it comes to fostering physical and ontological security.

Throughout this book I use the term 'security gap' to refer to two different dimensions of the unequal distribution of security among citizens. The first dimension consists of the gaps that exist in relation to what differently situated citizens in a given society are able to access as forms of security (the comparative perspective). Although I will spend some time discussing this aspect of social inequality in subsequent chapters, it is not the sole focus of this book. I am also interested in the second dimension, which is the gap that exists between the ideal state of personal security desired by citizens – in this case, homeless citizens – and their current lived reality (the subjective perspective). This second, subjective dimension is discussed primarily in chapter 6, where I examine what homeless citizens have to say about security and their personal experiences of and thoughts, feelings, and beliefs about insecurity and themselves as citizens leading insecure lives.

If security is the key benefit of citizenship – and at this time of writing this would appear to remain the case – then how ought we to interpret the existence of sizeable gaps in security acquisition and provision among groups of citizens? I suggest that, regardless of whether one is employing traditional conceptions of citizenship or taking the 'active citizen' as the yardstick with which to measure, we can arrive at no other conclusion than that those with minimal protections against violence, theft, economic exploitation, and other criminal threats can only be seen as inhabiting a space of lesser citizenship.

In making this argument, I am keenly aware of Mariana Valverde's (2001) admonishment that we ought not to treat security as an objective 'thing' of which one can have too little or too much. Instead, she argues, we need to recognize it for what it is: a temporally bounded, subjective state. She further contends that it would be preferable for scholars to treat security as an 'ideal,' and one that does not lend itself easily to calculation and predictability. While I can see significant merit to this line of reasoning – quantifying security is not, after all, like pouring sugar into a measuring cup – it remains the case that we can still say meaningful things about proximity to an individual or social ideal by asking people how they see their current position in relation to this desired state, and through comparatively assessing positions within and across groups. In the case of those who are homeless, employing both evaluative methods tells us that homeless citizens experience a security gap that is empirically demonstrated by their inability to access forms of security to prevent criminal victimization, forms of security that other social groups routinely access. From asking homeless people how they feel about their inability to access or possess forms of security, as well as their experiences of victimization, we can begin to put together a picture of what security means to members of this population and how closely this perception approximates their ideal security state.

2 Homelessness and Criminal Victimization

Robbed. You've been sleeping in places and you got robbed.
– Homeless man, Edinburgh

Marianne wanted to introduce me to someone. It was 2008 and Marianne Quirouette and I were in Edinburgh working on an evaluative study of a Scottish police program aimed at increasing reporting of victimization by homeless victims (Huey and Quirouette 2010b). She pointed to the sidewalk ahead and I saw a young woman begging there. We walked over, knelt down, and exchanged some brief pleasantries with her before excusing ourselves to continue on. As we walked, Marianne explained that this was the person she had interviewed the previous day, the one who had described to Marianne the experience of having been sexually assaulted and 'left for dead.'

Unfortunately, for many homeless citizens, the experience of being criminally victimized is far too common. Even such extreme cases as presented above are not unusual; indeed, some scholars have suggested that the instrumental and expressive use of violence within homeless populations is so frequent that violence is 'part of the homeless culture' (Ravenhill 2008: 166). Still others, myself included, note that crimes against the homeless citizen are committed not only by those from within their communities but also by 'outsiders' (Huey 2007; 2010). Both forms are significant contributing factors to their insecurity.

In the pages that follow, I explore the range of forms of criminal victimization that homeless residents experience – from petty theft and economic swindles to sexual assaults and murder. I present data on these criminal threats in order to provide the reader with a sense of the size and scope of the security gap that homeless citizens must grapple with. To aid in this process, in the next section I draw on comparative work by other researchers which reveals the extent to which homeless citizens are disproportionately victimized by crime. Then, to flesh out in further detail the nature of those crimes, in subsequent sections I explore both economic and violent crimes, drawing primarily on data collected from the 2003, 2007, and 2008 studies I conducted.

Rates of Criminal Victimization

The people who get victimized the most in the community are most often people who have the least.

– Service provider, Vancouver

One of the most significant problems confronting researchers on homelessness is the fact that we often lack detailed knowledge about issues that face this population. This is no less the case with respect to criminal victimization: while criminologists are aware of the volume of unreported crime with respect to offences in the general population, the 'dark figure of crime' becomes a veritable black hole when discussing crimes committed against homeless citizens. This black hole is a result of two factors. First, homeless citizens tend not to be represented within government surveys of crime and victimization because they do not have stable housing, frequently lack access to telephones, and often live more or less transient lives (Wardhaugh 2000; Pain and Francis 2004; Kohm 2006). Second, crimes against the homeless citizen are often uncounted within police or other criminal justice statistics because they go unreported by either the victim or witnesses (Huey 2007; Novac et al. 2007; Rosenfeld, Jacobs, and Wright 2003; McCarthy, Hagan, and Martin 2002; Wardhaugh 2000; Anderson 1999).

As a consequence of the above factors, the bulk of knowledge of victimization that we do have in relation to homeless citizens has come from independent studies conducted by researchers in the field. Some scholars have utilized surveys, while others have conducted in-depth qualitative studies of local homeless populations – with the result that we have a patchwork quilt of information regarding criminal victimization of those who are homeless. From this patchwork of data, some interesting general patterns emerge. First, it appears that homeless citizens tend to experience disproportionately high rates of victimization (Novac, Hermer, Paradis, and Kellen 2007; Lee and Schreck 2005;

Waccholz 2005; Evans and Forsyth 2004; Whitbeck, Hoyt, Yoder, Cauce, and Paradise 2001; Hagan and McCarthy 1997; Fitzpatrick, Le Gory, and Ritchey 1993). Second, one's chances of being victimized increase with length of time spent on the streets (Kipke, Simon, Montgomery, Unger, and Iversen 1997; Whitbeck, Hoyt, and Yoder 1999; Whitbeck et al. 2001).

In relation to the first fact – that homeless citizens are particularly vulnerable to criminal victimization – some researchers have established comparative benchmarks in order to demonstrate the extent of the problem. In one such study, Jana Jasinski and her colleagues (2010) compared the results of a survey of 737 homeless women in Florida to results obtained from the National Violence Against Women Survey (NVAWS) (2000).[1] What these researchers found was that their sample of homeless women consistently scored higher on various measures of victimization. For example, 56 per cent of the women they surveyed had experienced a rape or attempted rape compared to 18 per cent of respondents in the NVAWS study (ibid.). Whereas 50 per cent of the national sample stated that they had been physically assaulted at some point in their lives, 75 per cent of homeless women had been a victim of a physical assault (ibid.). Homeless women also reported higher rates of various forms of intimate partner violence (IPV), including stalking and physical assaults (ibid.).

Other studies have revealed similar results. In their sample of homeless individuals in Alabama surveyed for the period of 1986–7, K. Fitzpatrick et al. (1993) found that the rate at which their respondents had been victims of robbery, assault, and larceny was four times the rate reported in the National Crime Survey for the same time period. In an unusual cross-country comparison, Australian researchers compared rates of 'trauma' experienced by Sydney's homeless population to similar rates found within the U.S. general population (Buhrich, Hodder, and Teesson 2000). What they noted was that, in Sydney, 'homeless men were at particular risk for lifetime physical assault and rape; homeless women at particular risk for lifetime physical assault, physical threats, witnessing a trauma event, sexual molestation and rape' (ibid.: 964). When they compared their results to the U.S. general population, they found that in Sydney 'homeless women appear to be at an eightfold risk of lifetime experience of physical threats and assault, while homeless men report a 15-fold increased risk of rape' (ibid.: 964). In a 2003 study, Margot Kushel and her colleagues examined rates of victimization in their sample of approximately 2,600 homeless and marginally housed adults in San Francisco in comparison to estimated rates of similar offences in the general population. What they found was that their homeless sample experienced higher rates of both sexual and physical assault:

> For women, we found an annual rate of approximately 10% as compared with rates ranging from 2.5 per 1000 to 5% per year in non-homeless women. Most data on sexual assault in the general population are lifetime rates, estimates of which range from 13% to 25%. Among men, the difference was even greater; in the general population, annual rates are estimated at 0.3 per 1000. The rates of sexual assault among men in our study were higher than most estimates among women in the general population. Rates of physical assault in our study were also much higher than population norms. Because assault is more common in younger persons, the scarcity of subjects younger than 20 years in our study makes our findings more striking and suggests that homelessness eliminates age-related protections against physical assault. [2003: 2496]

In other research, rates of victimization among homeless youth have been compared to those of similarly aged victims surveyed within the general population, and here again we see significant differences in offence rates across populations, as well as differences in the types of offences committed. For example, in surveying homeless youth in Toronto, S. Gaetz, B. O'Grady, and K. Buccieri (2010) found that 76 per cent of their sample had been victimized at least once within the past twelve months, with almost 73 per cent reporting experiences of multiple victimization. As these authors note, 'this is an extremely high rate of criminal victimization, when compared to housed youth in the general population' (ibid.: 2). When the researchers looked at types of offences reported, they noted another remarkable difference: in contrast to the general public, which is more likely to report having been a victim of property crime, homeless youth surveyed were more likely to have been the victim of a violent personal-injury offence (ibid.). Indeed, they note that nearly 64 per cent of respondents cited at least one incident of violent victimization (ibid.).

Comparisons of victimization rates between homeless citizens and those who are marginally housed also yield differences. When they compared data from those who are homeless to data obtained from marginally housed citizens, Kushel and her team (2003) found that homelessness itself was a significant factor in increasing rates of victimization. However, although the marginally housed report fewer experiences of victimization than those citizens who are without steady access to shelter, when their rates of victimization are compared to those found within the general population, it appears that the marginally housed are also significantly affected by criminal victimization (Kushel et al. 2003).

In essence, what we can draw from these studies is that one's chances of being victimized – both physically and sexually – increase without access to stable housing.

Theft and Other Economic Offences

Theft … it happens all the time here.

– Homeless male, Toronto

Other studies suggest that the most common form of victimization reported by homeless citizens is theft of personal property (Lee and Schreck 2005; Evans and Forsyth 2004; Coston and Finckenauer 2004). This is no less the case in my own work. When respondents in each of my own studies were asked about victimization, petty thefts were identified as a common problem (Huey 2007; Huey and Berndt 2008; Huey and Quirouette 2009). As a homeless male in Toronto puts it, 'everybody pretty much gets stuff stolen from them.' His views are echoed by a shelter worker in Montreal, who explains that bags, clothes, and other personal items disappear as soon as the owner's back is turned. A fellow in Toronto had his backpack stolen: 'I lost my ID all of it. I lost my brand new cell phone, CD player, all that.' Despite security precautions within facilities, the view of one shelter resident is common: 'I see a lot of theft, even in this area here. People come in with stuff and they make friends, and then they're looking around for their stuff the next day' (Huey and Quirouette 2009: 35). That objects should go missing is not surprising, a female shelter resident in Toronto explains: 'At some of the other shelters, they might have thirty-five beds to a room. So, whatever you have in there is pretty much open to theft. There is a lot [of that] going on.' Nor is anyone immune from petty theft: an elderly female shelter resident in Toronto had a radio stolen out of her walker. This woman blames herself because knowledge of theft in shelters is common within the community: 'My fault; I was fully aware. I left it alone for not even five minutes … I should have known.' A police officer in Toronto agrees that theft is a problem generally, but suggests that it is particularly rampant within youth facilities: 'In shelters for youth, there's so much thievery going on that it's not even considered a big thing among them.'

Although vandalism does occur within homeless communities, it appears to be an offence more frequently affecting local service providers and businesses than homeless citizens themselves. Thus, most inter-viewees had little to say about vandalism, although two community-service workers in Vancouver did cite instances of vandalism. In one case, references were made to the fact that a neighbour's residence had been vandalized during a break-and-enter. In the other, a shelter worker spoke of how some of her clients used to deliberately commit property crimes at her facility. This service provider was making the point that not all property crime is predatory; indeed, she noted that sometimes homeless citizens commit petty crimes as a way of getting medical or addiction-related treatment or regular shelter. As she explained:

> Used to be that property crime was a way to get inside. I've had people years ago that would bust my windows and wait for the police to show up so they could spend the weekend in jail. But, yesterday, I had a guy who busted up some of my walls and he'd come back and he said, 'Why don't you charge me?' And I said, 'Well, I don't think we'd go anywhere with that. I may have to see. You know, if I have to go through the process of a civil suit, what do you got that you're going to pay to make up to the building anyways? The best I can get out of you is some time where you might be spending some time serving as a volunteer in my kitchen doing the dishes. And if you want to go there that's fine with me!' And he said, 'You should charge me with mischief because you were in sight and there was the other officer … there's an officer right there, you can get him to charge me.' I said, 'They're not going to bust you for mischief, it's damage. It becomes a civil matter.' And what he was really angry for is he can't get into treatment.

This service provider's experiences are not unusual. In Edinburgh, a homeless man advises that 'some of the people here, if you are going to report them, jail is a home away from home anyways. That's what half the guys in there will say.' I once met a young man in Vancouver's Downtown Eastside who was HIV positive and out on parole after a lifetime of being in and out of prison and juvenile institutions. Feeling that it would be better to be in prison, with regular meals, a bed, and medical treatment, he intended to commit another crime in order to be returned to prison.

Those who are homeless are also uniquely vulnerable to certain forms of financial scams that frequently occur within the geographical spaces they inhabit. While conducting research in Vancouver's DTES, I inter-viewed a senior police officer with many years of experience working in this impoverished community. This officer has spent considerable time trying to combat the fraudulent activities that take place within the hotels and bars that dot the area. One of the scams he identified involves Single Resident Occupancy (SRO) hotels that are provided cheques by the provincial government in order to secure monthly accommodation for benefit recipients. What the hotel owners permit the residents to do is to exchange their guaranteed accommodation for a substantially reduced sum of cash, so that the hotel can re-rent the room. The officer explains the scheme as follows:

> Do you know how it works? If you're able to come into my hotel, I'll give you half your rent cheque in money and you go out and use. So you bring in $325, I'll give you $163. You got out and use that on drugs. It keeps you going for 3 days ... I haven't given you anything. You aren't staying in the hotel. You've sold your place ... The hotels are ripping users off left, right and centre, because they're stealing legitimate housing. They're enabling you to go out and use drugs and get into risky behaviour. You're doing that; you're being used. You're giving it up because your drug need is so high ... I looked at one hotel, and in one room at this hotel, they had six cheques issued to one room. This room should've made 325, times six, and there's a seventh person in there. That's how much social welfare money went into it, for this one piece of shitty little room. You would've been charged by the Humane Society for having a dog in that room. About two thousand dollars went where? It went right into the slumlord's money and he provided nothing.

This officer's frustrations are voiced by another long-time veteran officer in the DTES, who notes that enforcement activities do little to halt such activities: 'There was one meeting where the city prosecutor was bragging about levelling a fine of $5,000 against the owners of the hotel. I just laughed. I said, "$5,000? They're laughing at you. That's just a cost of doing business for them. They can write that off." They're making a fortune off illegal scams at those hotels. Their standards are absolute garbage. You go in there and it's disgusting. Our so-called health standards are so low that all these owners know what they have to do to keep them above the standards. There's so many different scams, frauds, going on.' A shelter resident in Toronto advises that, when landlords 'take advantage of people' in such scams, the mentally ill are frequently among those victimized.

SRO hotels also engage in what is often little more than illegal taxation of residents by charging 'guest fees' whenever an occupant has a visitor to their room. The reason cited for these fees is that the hotel provides bedding to each room, which might require additional laundering if tenants receive guests. A SRO occupant in San Francisco's Tenderloin district explains these fees in the following terms: 'The only people that served was drug dealers. It served them because you had to have money to come see them. They didn't have people knocking on their door constantly, and it served the hotel owners because they didn't pay the desk clerks. The desk clerk's salary came from the guest fees.' Regular renters and their visitors are, however, often unable to pay fees or have to make sacrifices in order to have privacy with friends and family. Indeed, one woman noted that she and her boyfriend had used a significant portion of their limited funds to pay guest fees, which placed their relationship under both financial and emotional strain. In response to complaints about visitor fees, some cities, including San Francisco, have passed municipal by-laws prohibiting their collection by hotels. However, as an interview with a representative from San Francisco's city hall makes clear, the question of whether such laws are actually enforced remains open: '[We] passed a law that bans the collection of visitor fees in SRO hotels which is common practice. We actually wrote it into the Police Code ... I don't know if we've done any specific hearing or follow-up to find out how successful it is.'

Another financial scam that affects some homeless citizens involves 'under-the-table' employment at local hotels and bars for marginal, if any, wages. In Vancouver, police conducted a survey of 'problem businesses' in the DTES and, according to a senior officer, concluded that '100 per cent of the staff in the hotels were not receiving legitimate wages,' nor were the '40 or 45 per cent working in the bars.' In some instances, hotel staff are paid about two dollars an hour or a package of cigarettes, whereas bars hire known alcoholics who are willing to work solely for tips and beer money. A police officer explains the scam: 'What happens is if you come and work for me, you get the equivalent of about two beer an hour. A beer in a bar? A couple of bucks? You're on welfare, so you're marginal as it is. You make a little bit of tip money or you can have a couple of beer, which costs me about 50 cents a glass. So I'm paying you the equivalent of about a buck an hour.'

Sometimes the perpetrators of financial scams are family members of the victim. One case police investigated was that of an elderly woman who had been put out on the street by her son. One of the officers involved explains: 'She was eighty-two. And she got out on the street because her son, who was a crack addict, got her out of her apartment because he could get more money if he put her out on the street. He was managing all of her affairs.' As is the case with victimization of this population more generally, economic scams involving the homeless citizen frequently remain unreported and therefore usually generate little, if any, official response. In this particular instance, the elderly woman was fortunate in that a young police constable saw her on the streets, enquired as to why she was without shelter, and brought her situation to the attention of a senior officer.

Assaults and Other Violent Offences

I was strangled. I almost died.

– Homeless woman, Vancouver

Homeless citizens are frequent targets of harassing behaviour – from verbal abuse to intimidation and threats (Wardhaugh 2000; Wachholz 2005; Huey 2007). Such experiences are particularly common when they are 'hanging out' or begging in public spaces adjacent to nightlife venues. For example, beggars in the Cowgate and Grassmarket areas of Edinburgh's Old Town relate stories of verbal and physical harassment at the hands of young drunk males who come to party in the local bars. It is also not unusual for those who are panhandling to report having people coming up to them to harass and try to steal their money. For instance, a fellow in Edinburgh offers the following story: 'Like this one time I was sitting right in the centre of Edinburgh on the new steps leading down to the train station. So I'm sitting there with my harmonica and this guy came down. "Ah, you're begging!" "Uh, I never asked you for anything." So he picked up my hat – there must have been like seventy pence in it – put them in his pocket, threw my hat and said, "Start again."'

As is the case with their adult counterparts, homeless youth also experience routine harassment and abuse. A service provider in Vancouver explains that 'people will spit at them. Or throw change at them.' A youth worker similarly notes that it is not unusual for panhandling youth to have strangers shout derogatory comments at them, such as 'You bum. You lowlife. Get a job.'

Harassment of those who are homeless often turns to physical violence. In Edinburgh, 'rough sleepers' – those who sleep outdoors – offer stories of having been woken up by drunk patrons of the nearby bars. One service provider notes of his clients, 'They're trying to beg, they quite

Photograph 2.1 Homeless panhandler and Christmas shoppers (Toronto)

often get beaten up or robbed by night clubbers, groups of young folk out for a good time, been drinking. "Well here's somebody, let's have some fun"' (Huey 2007: 45). When one rough sleeper is asked about his experiences of such behaviour, he notes that trying to defend himself from these attacks is often useless because, if the police are called, this can sometimes leads to his receiving the blame for the incident:

Q: I know that a lot of crime that's committed around here is drunken idiots coming out of …
A: Lap dancing clubs. The strip clubs down the road.
Q: So you're skippering in Greyfriars, a couple of drunken lads would come along and …
A: Start trouble and the homeless person gets the blame for it. Society looks at you like you're the troublemaker.

Homeless individuals in both Toronto and Vancouver report similar experiences of being assaulted by partygoers who visit the bars and nightclubs lining each city's downtown core. In Vancouver, a police officer put the matter bluntly, 'Street people get shit kicked at 3:00 in the morning because they're sleeping in a lane. Some drunk who lives in Abbotsford[2] walking down there after partying, lays the boots to him' (Huey and Quirouette 2009: 37). Similarly, according to Toronto police, rough sleepers may be 'kicked in the head while they're sleeping.' A police officer who works in this city's entertainment district – where much of the city's nightlife is densely concentrated in a small geographical space – states that he and other officers routinely advise homeless people to leave the area before the bars close. As this officer explains of the club-goers who pour into the streets at closing: 'Sometimes they're very nice to [those panhandling], they'll throw money at them, or sometimes they're just mean drunks and they'll use them as a soccer ball.' Another officer states that he's seen cases where young male partiers 'get drunk,' find a homeless victim, and 'take whatever money they have, and then punch them and beat them up.'

Robberies of homeless citizens are also common, although these appear to be more frequently perpetrated by those within the homeless community. 'Often we hear consistent stories about one day, they go to the bank,' a shelter worker in Toronto says of his clients. 'A guy might know their pattern, and they end up getting robbed' (Huey and Quirouette 2009: 16). In Scotland, the practice is referred to as 'taxing.' A service provider explains that 'the government taxes you' and so those who can 'will tax the weaker element,' adding, 'If they've got drink, if they've got money, other people will take it from them.' In Toronto, a homeless female was robbed at knife point for ten dollars and a homeless male in that same city was forced to relinquish twenty dollars to a mugger. Often intimidating gestures and threats of violence are sufficient to ensure the production of money or goods. In other instances, victims are physically assaulted, as occurred to the friend of a woman in Toronto: 'There's a person I know. His name is Wizard,[3] and he was robbed at my place, where they sell drugs. He's walking through there and had his watch. They tried taking his watch, his money, some other things. He's walking through because he lives around that area. Nobody ever hurt Wizard before, and he got the shit kicked out of him. He ended up in the hospital. Fractured neck, fractured head.'

When weapons are used, victims are likely to say that they had been threatened or attacked with a knife, although one man reported having been robbed by a man wielding a piece of wood. In the following story, an elderly homeless man in Toronto relates his experience of having been robbed: 'Friday I was moving from here and had my money stashed at my friend's place. I came home at five in the morning and got attacked from behind ... the guy that did that to me, he's been my friend for three years. Three years I've known this guy, been really close, a lot of fun together, and then he pulls this. There was no friendship, this guy's just a praying mantis, waiting for the right time to come along ... I thought I was smart by leaving [the money] at my friend's place. It was a set-up. They were watching and waiting for me. He set it up. I'm certain he set it up.'

Much of the economic and social life of impoverished communities is based on a calendar that is set by government offices that disperse benefit cheques. In Vancouver's DTES, the last Wednesday of the month – known locally as 'welfare Wednesday' – is a much anticipated day for cheque recipients and robbers alike. When asked about violence in the DTES, a Vancouver police officer responds, 'Usually what's going on down here is, like on a welfare day, people will get drunk and roll each other for their cheques.' In Toronto, a service provider notes, 'We hand out what's called PNA – Personal Needs Allowance – and what happens sometimes is that they know which day we hand those out ... then all of a sudden there will be people waiting around for "Joe" and "Fred," and then they rob them and run off.' One enterprising client of a mental-health clinic in Edinburgh was targeting other members of a drop-in group. As a police officer explains, 'people's levels of schizophrenia ranged from debilitating to those who functioned extremely well ... [she] spent two years robbing her friends, going through the group, targeting the most vulnerable individuals she could find, and then stealing as much as she could possibly get ... all she did was rob people.'

Money is not always the motive for robbery. In many instances, victims are targeted because they are believed to be holding drugs. In response to a question about robbery, a homeless male in Toronto states, 'Picking people for their dope. You see that every day around here.' Police are also aware of this, as an officer notes: 'You have people who are preyed upon by the stronger elements in their community. It happens all the time, be they man or woman. It happens a lot of times over drugs, it happens over territories, it happens over property, it happens over a ton of stuff.'

Physical assaults are also depressingly common within homeless communities (Goodman and Dutton 1996; Evans and Forsyth 2004; Ravenhill 2008). 'I've seen people get beat up,' a homeless male in Toronto states matter-of-factly when asked about crime in his neighbourhood. Often such assaults are a response to an outstanding debt

over money or drugs. For example, in Vancouver drug dealers sometimes cut the hair of female addicts who owe them money (Huey 2007).
The rationale is simple: ownership of long hair being a prized female
attribute in the DTES, women will seek to avoid this 'punishment' by
not 'skipping out' on paying debts owed (ibid.). A community-service
provider who works with women in the DTES explains this form of
assault as follows: 'What these dealers are doing at Oppenheimer Park
with the women who have outstanding debts, you'll see a lot of women
with short cropped hair. They're stripping these women down and cutting it off as forms of punishment and intimidation. There's ten girls
around the park that all have really short hair and uneven cut and that's
why. Because they have drug debts. I've talked to some of the women
and I've said, "Wow, you're managing to keep your hair." And they're
like, "I have to. This is my hair. I'm a woman."'

Drug debts are also frequently settled by threats, beatings, and stabbings. After having just paid off a dealer in response to his threats to
'shank' her boyfriend for unpaid debts, a homeless woman living in
Toronto discovered that her boyfriend, André,[4] had racked up further
debt, leading to another round of threats:

> I go, 'I'll take a $200 credit.' He sells it to me, writes it down. In a month,
> I'll pay. André is down at the other end … he gets $1,000 front without me
> knowing. Then I didn't know he owed the other [guy] $500 from before, so
> I get a phone call from this guy, a dealer, and he turns around and goes,
> 'You guys owe me $1,500'… I go, 'I bought $200 off you.' He goes, 'Your
> boyfriend, he took it. Therefore you guys owe me. You're his girl, therefore
> you're together.' 'I go, 'What if I break up with him?' 'Well, still you got it
> before you broke up.' I go, 'Catch me if you can, okay?' He goes, 'I'll use a
> gun on you' … Last time it happened this guy was real rough. We had to
> pay him.

Drug-related extortion is also an issue, with younger people threatening
to assault those who don't buy from them. A woman in Toronto who
was down to her last ten dollars was forced to give up her money when
confronted with such a threat: 'The kids are beating people up if they
don't buy dope off them. I walk through, they go, "You got money?" I
go, "Yeah." "Buy something!" "No." They go, "Fine, we'll hit you then."
I'll say, "I only got ten bucks." "That's fine, you're not leaving this thing
until you give ten."'

Sometimes an assault is simply the result of a verbal altercation or other misunderstanding between two or more parties (Ravenhill 2008). When asked about assaults, a woman in Montreal reports that 'there's a lot of jealousy and ah … in some situations, so sometimes I've been in fights and stuff like that, but over stupid stuff.' Another woman interviewed in the same shelter spoke of having been assaulted by a strange man who was looking for a cigarette: 'I was walking down the street and this guy came up to me and said, "Do you got a cigarette?" and I went, "No, I don't," and he beat me up. And he was on a bicycle and he started punching me you know, and my arm wasn't well yet, and I had an accident. He started punching my arm … someone beat you up, you know, cause you don't have a cigarette' (Huey and Berndt 2008: 185). A woman in Vancouver cited several instances of having been 'beaten up on the street' by other females with whom she was engaged in minor disputes (Huey and Quirouette 2009). In other cases, assaults appear to be unprovoked or for no known reason. For instance, a police officer in Toronto cites an incident that had recently occurred: 'Talking to a young boy last week, and he was in a shelter, just walked by this guy, and this guy punched him for no reason. Unprovoked, just punched him.' Both police and service providers cite drugs and alcohol as probable factors in such situations. To illustrate, a service provider in San Francisco shared an incident in which an individual at his facility 'was high on speed' and 'threatening people … disrupting the place.' As the service provider explains, this individual 'was obviously fucked up and like very not reality-oriented,' and his aggressive postures were seen as threatening to other clients.

Assaults by a sexual partner are also common, as intimate partner violence remains a significant issue within many homeless communities. 'My ex tried to break my neck,' a woman in a wheelchair in Vancouver states. 'He grabbed me by the jaw, crushed it in here' (Huey and Quirouette 2010: 284). When asked about victimization, a woman in Vancouver cites her experience of being stalked and assaulted by an ex-fiancé. 'He follows me down the street, he's my personal stalker,' she says. 'I can't even be safe in the community. It sucks.' Service providers who work with homeless women acknowledge that IPV remains a huge problem. For women who escape their abusers, many are subsequently stalked. A service provider who works with Aboriginal women provides one such example: 'One of the sisters was having problems with her ex … he was stalking her.' In discussing the problem of unreported

IPV among those who are homeless, a senior police officer in Toronto describes the issue as 'phenomenal,' adding, 'I guarantee you they do not come forward. It is just an accepted practice of their life. It is what they are used to and accustomed to.' A woman interviewed in Edinburgh explains that she didn't report the abuse that she received from her husband because 'he would've killed me. It was safer not to, to keep taking the beatings.'

Since the 1980s, when deinstitutionalization led to the literal dumping of the mentally ill onto the streets and into impoverished communities, individuals with mental illness have been among the most frequently victimized subgroups within homeless populations (Sullivan, Burnam, Koegel, and Hollenberg 2000; Schrek and Lee 2005). Indeed, one study found that, while the rate of non-violent criminal victimization of mentally ill homeless respondents was similar to that of the general population, the rate of violent criminal victimization experienced – including assaults, rapes, and robbery – was two and a half times greater (Hiday, Swartz, Swanson, Borum, and Wagner 1999). These researchers note that younger people and African Americans with mental illness tended to have higher rates of reporting for both violent and non-violent offences (ibid.). A study of homeless mentally ill women in the United States found that participants' lifetime risk 'for violent victimization is so high that rape and physical battery are normal experiences' (Goodman, Dutton, and Harris 1995: 474). Such statistics are supported by the lived experiences of those who live and work within homeless communities. For instance, a service provider in San Francisco describes a client who was 'very, very mentally ill and in a state of being utterly psychotic'; she feared that if the client, 'who had been assaulted so many times, it was just horrible,' was not hospitalized, 'she was going to get killed.' A homeless fellow in Toronto advises, 'I've seen a lot of people victimized, like the mentally ill ... people with mental illness are preyed upon here, you bet.' A Vancouver police officer notes that the situation can be dangerous for those who end up in the city's DTES: 'In this area we have 1,100 mental illness patients registered with Strathcona Mental Health. A thousand of them are double-diagnosed, mentally ill and they are drug addicted. You're talking about a really marginalized community. On top of that the estimates are 3,000 to 3,500 mentally ill people living in this area that aren't taking their meds ... they become victims.'

Rates of sexual abuse and assault are also high in homeless communities, with much of this victimization remaining unreported to authorities (Maher et al. 1996; Kushel et al. 2003; Evans and Forsyth 2004).

Indeed, over the years women interviewed have cited numerous experiences of such forms of victimization, ranging from sexual harassment to sexual abuse to abduction and brutal sexual assault. Sexual harassment is so prevalent on the streets – from men both within and outside the local community – that many women say that they 'dress down' or act inconspicuously while in public in order to avoid unwanted male attention (Huey and Berndt 2008). For example, when asked about sexual harassment, a woman in Montreal says, 'I will get slandered like, "How much for a blow job?" You know, screaming at me on the street … it scares me.'

Transgendered women interviewed report receiving a lot of sexual harassment on the streets. 'I either get one extreme or the other,' a transgendered female says in San Francisco. 'I either get violent reactions out on the street or I get … sexual comments and following.' To illustrate this point, she notes: 'I was threatened, sort of, yesterday. I was on my way to the library, which is really not this area … a belligerent person came up to me and started calling me names and basically started to voice a threat. I ignored him until he stopped following me.' Similarly, another transgendered woman reports being subjected to sexually threatening language and behaviour from strange males, actions that stopped only when she acquired a lover who served as her constant protector. Other research has also shown that trans-identified youth and adults are vulnerable to both physical and sexual assault (Kushel et al. 2003).[5]

Sexual harassment, abuse, assault, and exploitation are significant problems that are experienced by homeless women across the age spectrum. Indeed, studies suggest that elderly homeless females are just as likely to experience physical and sexual abuse as homeless women in other age groups (Goodman, Dutton, and Harris 1995). One sad example is provided by the story of 'Sally,'[6] a street drinker whose story is told by a community-service provider:

> She was a lady in her fifties who had a lot of physical health problems and mental health problems … chain smokes, likes a drink. Wasn't supposed to drink because of physical problems, diabetes, she was incontinent … She was always filthy, stained … She was a really sad, sad old lady, but she was also a very nice old lady. You could sit and talk to [her]. She would love you, and wanted love. There was a guy called Willie[7] who was a street drinker [alcoholic] in his sixties, maybe seventies … Willie was getting Sally drunk and taking her up to his flat over here. He'd take her back up there, have her drunk, do his business with her. She was lonely, she liked

company … he was using her, and she wasn't in a position to really say no because of her mental health, because of her loneliness …[8] about four months ago Sally died in Willie's flat. What happened was that Willie got her drunk again, took her up to the flat, and she had a massive heart attack in his bed. [Huey and Berndt 2008: 185]

Nor are homeless youth immune from sexual exploitation and abuse. In relation to females, I first became aware of exactly how vulnerable they are to sexual exploitation on the streets while interviewing three homeless teenagers (fifteen and sixteen years of age) panhandling on Vancouver's Granville Mall. Minutes prior to my sitting down to talk with them, two men had approached the girls offering to pay them for sex (Huey 2007). During the subsequent interview, the youths revealed that this was not an unusual occurrence and that other 'street kids' try to protect them from such predatory behaviour. Service providers advise that, for homeless youth, using sex as a means of survival often leads to their becoming victims of sexual exploitation. In Vancouver, there is a significant risk that some of the male and female youth who panhandle in the downtown core will end up in being exploited in the sex trade. A service provider who works with homeless youth notes that in the city's 'kiddie stroll' one can find 'sexually exploited' girls who are 'ten, eleven, twelve years old. They're dressed up in very adult clothes and they're doing very adult things, and are being exploited by adults.' A police officer who works with exploited youth in Vancouver observes: 'It doesn't take long for these kids to become hooked on drugs and after a couple of weeks of getting the free stuff, when they're hooked the pimps just basically say you need to work for that stuff now. And that's the beginning of the end. We're talking about kids that are eleven, twelve, thirteen years old, that aren't going to live to be twenty. By the time that they have an addiction to hard-core drugs, they've been in to high-risk behaviours, and their seroconversion rate is quite high for HepC and HIV, and the violence that happens on the street. It's very, very scary.' His partner adds: 'I think given the way the system has been working, it always ends up that the kids are the victims. They're being sexually abused and exploited and criminalized at the same time.' To illustrate the point further, one of the officers shares their collective experience of working with youth on the streets: 'We do know a couple of girls that mom saw the kid as basically a way of exploiting money out of the johns by saying, "Okay, well, it'll cost you a hundred bucks with me. How about 200 for the kid or 300?" And then mom and daughter become sort of a team in that sort of aspect and it's ugly, but it's true.' When asked

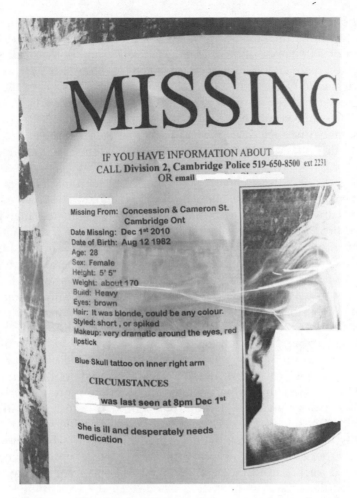

MISSING

IF YOU HAVE INFORMATION ABOUT
CALL **Division 2, Cambridge Police** 519-650-8500 ext 2231
OR email

Missing From: Concession & Cameron St.
               Cambridge Ont
Date Missing: Dec 1ˢᵗ 2010
Date of Birth: Aug 12 1982
Age: 28
Sex: Female
Height: 5' 5"
Weight: about 170
Build: Heavy
Eyes: brown
Hair: It was blonde, could be any colour.
Styled: short , or spiked
Makeup: very dramatic around the eyes, red lipstick

Blue Skull tattoo on inner right arm

CIRCUMSTANCES

was last seen at 8pm Dec 1ˢᵗ

She is ill and desperately needs medication

Photograph 2.2 Missing woman poster on a pole near homeless shelters (Toronto)

about the sexual exploitation of children and youth in Vancouver, a senior police officer advises that, when he worked frontline patrol, '[the] youngest kid I've taken off the street was eight. She was hooking.' A homeless man in Vancouver's DTES states that he has heard of multiple instances of women and girls being forced into the sex trade: 'girls being raped ... girls being kidnapped and put in some hotel and tricked out ... it's amazing, the crap that I've heard that goes on.'

Although other researchers have found that a number of homeless male respondents have been sexually assaulted (McIntyre 2005; McCreary 2001), none of the men interviewed in any of the studies I've conducted have cited experiences of sexual assault. However, service providers who work in the field of homelessness are aware of the existence of male victims. As a Toronto shelter worker explains, 'men are sexually assaulted and they don't report it.' A worker at a different shelter describes one such case: 'We had a guy that was raped up here ... on the fourth floor ... with a knife to his neck' (Huey and Quirouette 2009: 17).

As is the case with the general population, murder remains a relatively rare event among homeless populations. This is not to say, however, that murders do not happen. In one notable instance, a homeless man interviewed in a Toronto shelter in the 2008 study related his experience of having witnessed the murder of a close friend: 'I've seen my best friend killed over this word: goof. People use it too frequently around this place. Goof is just an idiot, but it has as much implication as being a rat ... I saw my best friend shot to death beside me. Right beside me. I was sitting beside him and if I hadn't rolled off my chair I would have got part of the shotgun blast too because somebody said that my friend called him a goof. No such thing happened, because I was with him all day. It was a setup ... He was nineteen years old. He was murdered because somebody said that he said he called him a goof, and it never happened.' Other individuals related incidents of having nearly lost their life through an attempted murder. A man in Edinburgh had been 'stabbed in the back of the neck by a four-inch steak knife.' He was lucky not only to be alive but to have recovered fully from his injuries. Had the knife penetrated 'two centimetres to the left, I would have been paralyzed for life from the neck down.' The Vancouver woman mentioned earlier whose ex-partner crushed her neck was attempting to strangle her: 'I almost died.'

Often homicides that occur are related to activities generated by the drug trade. While working in the DTES in 2003, fights over territory during a police crackdown on the local drug trade led to nights where the sounds of gunfire could be heard in and around the contested area of Oppenheimer Park. One area resident advised that, after the fighting began, a man was found dead on the steps of his building, his head bashed in – another casualty of the narcotics trade.

In terms of vulnerability to violent victimization, research suggests that two groups are particularly at risk: the mentally ill and sex-trade workers (Roche, Neaigus, and Miller 2005; Kushel, Evans, Perry, Robertson, and Moss 2003). For the latter group, participation in a criminalized, subsistence activity renders them particularly at risk of violence. Over the years, participants in sex-work activities have reported physical and sexual assaults, and community-service providers and police have related stories of clients who have been horribly victimized. So common are such incidents that one police officer in Toronto opined of those working the 'low track strolls' that 'they're being sexually assaulted every night, some have been murdered.' In support of this view, a service provider who works with homeless women in the sex trade says, 'We see the ladies that work on the streets, in the sex trade. They often come back, having been assaulted in some way.' Another advises that one of her clients had been found after a 'john slit her throat and left her to die.' The victim in this case was a transgendered woman who had been gang-raped before her assailants attempted to kill her.[9] In Toronto, an officer described working a homicide case where a sex worker 'was bludgeoned to death in one of our rear lanes where the prostitutes are, the dealers are, the addicted persons are … it's just a common track and she was beaten to death at four in the morning.' In Vancouver, a police officer notes that 'the prostitutes in the downtown core are so dependent on cocaine and heroin that they'll do anything to buy it. So we end up with perverts who come from the whole Lower Mainland to the downtown core and use [the women] as punching bags.' During my field research in 2003, women in the DTES, some of whom worked in or were associated with the area's sex trade, had been disappearing off the streets of Vancouver. It was subsequently discovered that many of those who had 'disappeared' had in fact been murdered by serial killer Willie Pickton.

Security?

The level of violence has escalated so much higher since then to where … before it was mostly users hanging out, more so than dealers, and now it's dealers on the street. Now I don't know where the dealers were before, whether they were in the bar or what, but now they're on the street and on the street with guns.

– Community-service provider, San Francisco

As the material presented in the preceding pages make evident, homeless citizens are vulnerable not merely to theft and various economic scams but also to violent victimization, including robbery, assault, and sexual violence. Indeed, not only are homeless citizens frequently victims of crime, but many have been victimized on multiple occasions and by multiple forms of crime. In elaborating in this chapter on the nature and scope of that victimization, I have endeavoured to begin the process of fleshing out aspects of the security gap this group of citizens face.

Comparisons of rates of victimization between homeless and non-homeless citizens offer a starting point to understanding this gap. We know, for example, that researchers have consistently found that homeless men, women, and youth are more likely to be victimized by crime than members of the general public (Fitzpatrick et al. 1993; Kushel et al. 2003; Jasinski et al. 2010). Comparisons alone are not, however, enough to provide a thorough understanding of the issues involved and their import for citizens. Thus, in order to give some meaning to these comparisons and the numbers cited, I also drew on my own research on the victimization of this population. Abstracting from interviews conducted with homeless men, women, youth, police, and community- service providers in five different cities, we begin to get a fuller sense of the types of victimization routinely experienced (I will have much more to say about the impact of these crimes on the homeless citizen in chapter 6).

With regard to victimization rates among those who are homeless, clearly their life situations – exposure to the streets, the need to find means of securing shelter or food, issues related to addiction, and so on – increase risk both individually and cumulatively. To understand the security gap, however, we need to recognize that risk is only one side of the security equation. Individual or collective risk of criminal victimization can be offset to a certain degree by actions taken to reduce it – that is, through access to and use of forms of security. Thus, if we want to get at the nature of the security gap, we must also consider what is available to the individual or the group to offset their risk, and what strengths and limitations are associated with various risk-aversion and/or security-promoting strategies.

Returning to the three modes of security provision discussed in the previous chapter, I reiterate the fact that homeless citizens currently remain more or less locked out of the private security market. What remains, then, is state-based modes of security, ostensibly available to all citizens, as well as private individual and collective forms of security. In the next chapter, I look at the former – the state as a source of security – and consider the extent to which, through the offices of the public police, the state and its agents are able to provide this resource for homeless citizens.

3 State-Based Security

To me the police are a necessary evil, nothing more than that. In a perfect society, we would not need policemen, but we live in an imperfect society so we need them. But it could be an awful lot better.

– Homeless male, Edinburgh

A line-up was forming outside the soup kitchen. I looked at various people in the line trying to determine whom I should approach first. I was uncomfortably aware that October in San Francisco had turned unseasonably warm. As I stood sweating and pondering my selection, I noticed a small, neat Hispanic man. I made eye contact, he smiled, and I approached him.

Roberto[1] was a middle-aged gay man living in one of the SRO hotels that dot the Tenderloin. I briefly explained my work to him, and he immediately agreed to be interviewed. He had had his place broken into several times by an ex-partner, who stole any valuables he had. According to Roberto, when the police arrived the first time he called, their response was, 'This is the Tenderloin and you're never going to get your stuff back.' To his chagrin, when he called to report another break-in, the police did not show up at all, so he stopped calling them. I asked Roberto if he was going to follow up on his police report and the following conversation ensued:

A: I just let it go because they weren't willing to, like, listen to me.
Q: If you had a problem now, would you call them?
A: No. I'd just kill the person [laughing] and then make sure that there were no witnesses and say, 'Can you prove it?'

Q: They'd say, 'Hey, it's a bad neighbourhood,' right?
A: [laughing] It could be anybody! And nobody saw me, so there.

Unfortunately, Roberto's experience is hardly unique.

Although legislators and the various arms of the criminal justice system play important roles in fostering conditions of physical security within the borders of a given state, it is the institution of the police that stands as 'the most visible and symbolically potent form of governance in the modern city' (Herbert 2001: 445). After all, it is the police who serve on the frontlines of the quest for social order and who have been granted exceptional powers in order to serve this cause, a cause deemed vital to the healthy functioning of the state and its citizens. As E. Bittner (1990 [1970]) documented some decades ago, citizens variously respect, recognize, and rely upon the police and their powers to aid the individual and collective pursuit of security. As Bittner also noted, the practice of mobilizing the police to respond to physical and other threats is 'more frequent in some segments of society than in others' (ibid.: 39). Roberto's experience, as discussed above, is instructive as to why this might be the case. Within this chapter, I explore homeless citizens' attitudes towards reporting victimization to the police and, in particular, why the 'original bargain' between the state and this group of citizens tends to disadvantage rather than benefit the latter.

Calling the Police

Q: If you were victimized, would you report it to the police?
A: If I had to. If I felt like I had no choice at all, I suppose I would. But
   I wouldn't get my hopes up that they would do anything that would help.
   Unless it was blatantly obvious and I had the evidence and they could
   come along and arrest the guy. But other than that, no.
                              – Interview with homeless male, Edinburgh

One of the manifest functions of criminal law is to bolster citizen security through the removal of threats to individuals and the social body. Not only is this an often imperfect method for creating individual and community security, it is also one that relies in large part on the willingness of citizens to report offences to police or other authorities – that is, to mobilize the machinery of the state (Black 1973). For most citizens, the decision to report an offence to authorities is a personal one, based on what the individual perceives as a desired outcome and the best means of achieving that outcome (Reiss 1971). Desired results may include the eradication of a threat, the cessation of continuing offences, redress for a wrong committed, and monetary recompense or the recovery of stolen objects, as well as access to medical, psychological, or other assistance. Other citizens may report an offence from a sense of public duty, feeling that by coming forward they are doing their part to prevent future victimization to others (Tarling and Morris 2010). Conversely, individuals may choose not to report because of issues of time, privacy, or other personal considerations, including a desire to be left alone by authorities or fear of retaliation. Various community and state-based reporting programs attempt to sway the decision-making process in favour of reporting on the ground that notifying the police of a crime represents the first step of a process that will enhance public safety. Indeed, the link between reporting and enhanced security is often made explicit in promotional materials extolling the virtues of crime reporting, as in the case of WeTip (2010), a non-profit crime-reporting organization that utilizes 'for a safer America!' as its tagline.

Research into the victimization of homeless citizens consistently finds that this section of the population under-reports (Ballintyne 1999; Wardhaugh 2000; Fischer 2004; Huey and Quirouette 2009, 2010; Novac et al. 2007; Roebuck 2008). However, although homeless victims and witnesses are often unwilling to report crimes to police, it should be made clear that lack of willingness to notify authorities of offences is not a universal condition. Some homeless citizens do seek assistance from the police: 'If I was victimized I would go to the police,' a man interviewed in Edinburgh says. 'I would ask the police for help.'

As is the case with the public more generally (Skogan 1976; Singer 1988; Laub 1997; Wood and Edwards 2005), when homeless citizens do report victimization it is because they deem the offence to be serious enough to merit an investment of their time and that of the police. Offences that respondents have said they would report include forcible entry, aggravated physical and sexual assault, and attempted murder. When a homeless man in Edinburgh was asked if he would report victimization to police, he replied in the negative. However, as the following excerpt from that same interview reveals, when he was asked about more serious offences, his response was very different:

Q: And what if it was a more serious crime, like if someone stabbed you or
    something?
A: I would call the police.

Q: You would call the cops?
A: Yeah, definitely.

The response above is not uncommon; when queried, an individual's response as to whether he or she would report to police was frequently based on an evaluation of whether the offence was seen as minor and therefore not worth 'the hassle.' For instance, an interviewee in Edinburgh feels that, if an offence is too petty, then 'I'm not going to bother.' I note that other respondents similarly use the word 'bother' to explain why they wouldn't report victimization to police, characterizing the reporting process either as a bother for themselves or as not worth the bother for police. As an example, when asked if he has ever reported experiences of being 'taxed' (mugged) to police, an elderly street drinker replies, 'I don't bother.' In response to a question as to the circumstances in which he might report victimization, a male shelter user in Toronto dismisses the idea of reporting to police what he perceives to be a non-issue: 'Just because someone gives me a punch in the face, that probably wouldn't be enough for me to [report]' (Huey and Quirouette 2009: 19). For this individual, a minor assault is not sufficient to be considered a criminal offence worthy of reporting. When one older fellow in Edinburgh was mugged and the incident was brought to the attention of the police by other parties, he opted to pretend that he didn't recognize his victimizer on the ground that the whole matter was too trivial to waste their time:

A: Well I must say, like in the past when I got mugged, I never bothered
    people.
Q: You never told?
A: Yeah, they showed me the photographs.
Q: Were the police helpful?
A: To an extent. It was a situation where I looked through the mug shots and
    I seen the person who did it but I didn't tell them.
Q: Oh.
A: When it comes to people who have done me a bad thing, I have a photo-
    graphic memory. I'll forget your name, but I'll never forget a face.
Q: What are the reasons why you didn't tell them? Is it because you didn't
    want to be a grass?
A: No, simple case of why take up police time and have them looking for this
    person, costing them a fortune, you know. And then what happens if they
    get taken to court, they get a fine or something like that?

Police are aware that victims are often not forthcoming about what has happened to them. 'Sometimes they know who it is,' an officer in Toronto says, 'sometimes they say they don't, and [they] probably do.'

Other reasons provided by homeless citizens for choosing not to report victimization to police frequently echo those heard from other members of the general public (Huey and Quirouette 2010; Jasinski et al. 2010), including embarrassment or shame over the offence, lack of confidence in police effectiveness, and the belief that nothing could or would be done by the criminal justice system (Skogan 1976; Kidd and Chayet 1984; Singer 1988; Davis and Henderson 1993). Several of those who hold negative views towards the notion of contacting the police state that their attitude is a consequence of dissatisfaction with the results of previous reporting attempts. For instance, a Vancouver woman asserts that she will no longer report crimes to the police because 'you get a report number and nothing gets done' (Huey and Quirouette 2009). Similar views were heard from a service provider in the Tenderloin who explains her lack of confidence in the police as a result of her own personal experiences with the reporting process: 'Have you ever reported a crime at a police station? It's ridiculous. They just go, "Okay, what's your name, etc." Like, you could have written this information down and given it to them. You didn't even need to talk to the guy. They don't like really look into it … They're like, "Well we can write a report …" And it's just like great, now there's another crime stat. Yah, that's helpful' (Huey 2007: 128). Another service provider in San Francisco states that his clients rarely report because 'people get demoralized,' adding, 'We have situations where people are seriously hurt and [the cases are] not prosecuted.'

As with domestic violence more generally, in some cases homeless victims do not come forward because they are unaware of resources available or come from cultures where IPV is not typically reported. A shelter worker explains that in Toronto 'we do have a lot of abused women who come to the shelter, and in their culture you just don't talk about it – you don't report it.' Such women end up at shelters because they 'realize that abuse isn't accepted here, and they don't have to deal with it anymore,' but they lack the support required to file a report with police.

While the reasons offered for not reporting victimization by homeless citizens often mirror concerns identified in the research literature more generally, significant differences can also be observed. One of these differences is that many homeless individuals experience multiple victimizations, and thus the experience of victimization can become normalized (Wardhaugh 2000). Indeed, a common theme within much of the research literature is the experience of high rates of victimization by homeless citizens *before* they ever enter the streets (Simons and Whitbeck 1991; Tyler et al. 2001; Paradise and Cauce 2002; McIntyre 2005). As a service provider in Toronto explains of her clients, they often don't report offences because of issues linked to 'low self-esteem and self-deprivation – being abused since they were children.' As a result, she suggests, their lives become repeating patterns of 'being victimized and victimizing others.'

There are, however, three other interrelated factors that inhibit reporting, factors that say much about the relationship of the homeless citizen to the state and its agents. These are citizen concerns related to: 1) antagonistic relations with police; 2) the individual's status (i.e., homeless, criminal); and 3) the operation of an anti-snitching code within street-based communities.

Relations with Police

I wouldn't send my worst enemies to the police. The people I hate more than anybody, I would not send to the police.

– Homeless man, San Francisco

For many of us, involvement with the police is, at best, marginal, limited to our receipt of speeding tickets or police response to a break-in at our home. In the daily lives of homeless citizens, the police play a much more significant role. After all, it is at the places the homeless citizen inhabits that police are often to be found, responding to calls, looking for suspects, monitoring disorder, moving beggars along, and so on. Further, as numerous researchers have documented, those who are homeless are also frequently the target of routine and extraordinary policing activities ('crackdowns'), so the presence of police is largely an inescapable fact of life for these citizens (Beckett and Herbert 2010; Harcourt 2001; Parenti 1999). As a downtown beat officer in Vancouver acknowledges, 'We're part of the streetscape' and so homeless citizens are 'used to seeing us.'

For most homeless citizens, police officers fall into one of two general types: interchangeable men and women in uniforms who are seen as objects of distrust; or individual, exceptional police officers who have become well known and trusted fixtures of the street scene. I have encountered both types. My exposure to the former first came from observing police officers in San Francisco routinely waking up sleeping homeless people and ordering them off the city's sidewalks in expectation of an influx of tourists for a big football game. I've also had direct experience of moving through a community – Vancouver's DTES – with the latter type, watching as local residents approached the beat officers in order to 'shoot the shit,' joke around, bum smokes, and so on. In relation to this group of officers, homeless residents are likely to say that they don't like the police, but that 'there are a few of them that are alright' (Huey 2007: 75) or that Constable So-and-So is 'a lovely man,' as one homeless woman in Edinburgh said of an officer in that city. Indeed, many of those who say that they would report victimization to police were careful to spell out that they would not report to just any police officer, instead identifying specific individuals they see as trustworthy. Other researchers have similarly referenced the often ambivalent nature of relationships between homeless citizens and the police. J. Wardhaugh (2000: 128), for example, notes that homeless young people will sometimes actively seek out police protection, 'preferring to accept any attendant risks of regulation in preference to the dangers presented to them by the public.'

More often than not, though, it is the homeless citizen who is viewed by members of the general public as a nuisance or a potential criminal threat. When this happens, demands are placed on police to regulate the presence of the homeless citizen in public and private spaces. For instance, police report that it is routine for them to receive calls from businesses that their customers are being subject to 'things like constant hassling by panhandlers.' As an officer in Vancouver explains, 'Okay, you've got a homeless guy living in your doorway. Who do you phone? You phone the cops.' Thus, as a frontline police supervisor in Toronto puts the matter, 'we are the enemy.' Police are viewed as such, he opines, 'because we are the ones that get the calls. We are the ones that have to go and move them along, give them tickets, arrest them.'

Certainly, in many instances, the presence of police in their daily lives is viewed by homeless men and women as an unwanted and unwarranted intrusion. These feelings are engendered by police enforcement activities that are seldom perceived as being for the benefit of homeless citizens within the community. Indeed, negative relations with police and/or negative beliefs or attitudes towards the police are among the most cited of barriers to reporting. A female shelter resident in Vancouver exemplifies the views of other citizens when she explains that she is

Photograph 3.1 Police sign advertising free meals to discourage panhandling (Vancouver)

unwilling to approach police officers because 'I could get that cop who is going to turn on me' (Huey and Quirouette 2009). Similarly, a homeless woman in San Francisco states that she wants police to 'have different trainings' because they 'still discriminate and I still don't trust them. Since I don't trust them, I don't know if they're going to be there to hurt me.' In Toronto, a service provider says of her clients, 'There is a real fear of the police, and whether it's real or not, it's real to them' (ibid.). Frequently, the cause of homeless citizens' lack of confidence in, fear of, and/or negative attitudes towards police is prior experience of police harassment and/or physical abuse.

Police harassment is a particularly common experience for many homeless citizens. Although it is often not illegal to sit on local city sidewalks, police drive by and tell panhandlers to get up and move on, as I once discovered when I tried to interview a couple of street youth on a Vancouver sidewalk. Harassment can also take the form of illegal stops and searches, as a Vancouver man describes below: 'We're at the bottle depot this morning taking some bottles in for one of the guys who's onsite here. Fishes cans so that he can support whatever he needs for the day. His coffee, whatever. Five cops approach a guy in the line at the bottle depot and shook him down for no reason. Five of them. They find nothing on him.' In Vancouver, both community-service providers and street youth themselves advise that it is not uncommon for the latter to be woken up by police in the middle of the night, when sleeping rough, and told by officers to move on. A youth worker explains his clients' experiences of the police as 'boots to the head or to the side, saying, "You can't sleep here."' Homeless Vancouver youth also speak of other forms of harassment by police, ranging from being moved along for no reason to receiving a 'starlight tour.'[2] One aggrieved youth describes his interactions with police as 'being fucking woken up and being fucking taken out to Sea to Sky Highway and fucking dropped off. Being taken out to fucking Abbotsford and dropped off.' Another young homeless male panhandling on Vancouver's Granville Street states that he has 'a lot of experience with the pigs. Really annoying. They give you a hard time lots of the time for just really sitting around. Or they see you on the street and they kick you off the street. You go in the back alleys and the kick you out of the back alleys. Basically they don't want you anywhere in the whole entire city, right? They just want you to just disappear off the whole face of the Earth, basically. It doesn't matter where you go the cops will tell you to move eventually.'

Vancouver's homeless youth are hardly alone in being moved from place to place, often without legal or other justification (Dordick 1997; Jasinski et al. 2010). In Edinburgh, being 'moved along' by police is a routine, if often disliked, aspect of street life for the city's panhandlers, street drinkers, and other homeless residents. When asked why he didn't think the police treated people well, a street drinker responds, 'They don't like 'em begging in the street.'

Q: Do they ask you to move on?
A: [Nods].

Such activities were observed first-hand during an interview with a female beggar near the Royal Mile. The man being moved by police was the boyfriend of the woman being interviewed.

Q: Why's he moving him?
A: Because he's too close to the bank. See where the bank is.
Q: Oh, that's the bank right there?

Photograph 3.2 Officer questions homeless man (Edinburgh)

A: Aye.
Q: Do they come and hassle you often?
A: Yup.

In many jurisdictions, police are able to utilize a host of city and state ordinances to ticket homeless residents for 'status offences,' such as those in San Francisco relating to camping, public urination or defecation, and panhandling. When the tickets remain unpaid, as they invariably do, bench warrants are issued for the individual's arrest, creating a mechanism whereby police can jail residents at almost any time (Huey 2007). State health codes allow police officers to confiscate possessions that are deemed 'health hazards' by officers, including bedrolls, blankets, and clothing (ibid.). Residents are of the view that not only is the issuing of tickets for status offences a discriminatory practice in and of itself, but that some officers discriminate against people of colour when handing out such tickets. A female SRO resident in San Francisco describes attending a food line where she observed police 'stopping certain people in the line to give them tickets' and that 'it was mostly like the Spanish and the black people.' Trespassing laws permit easy removal of homeless residents from various public and private spaces. So ubiquitous is their use as a policing tool to 'manage' the homeless citizen that, in a recent study of urban social exclusion in Seattle, Katherine Beckett and Steve Herbert (2010: 79) found that 'a third of all encounters between police officers and suspects identified as homeless begin with the investigation of an alleged trespass violation.' In the following story, a homeless male in San Francisco describes how his violation of a trespassing law precipitated ongoing harassment by a local police officer:

A: I got out in '92 on parole. I went back six times. I came over here because there's more opportunities over here than there is in Oakland. So I came over here. Anyway, during the course – I was going to computer class and I wasn't advanced – anyway, I was sleeping on the streets. I was sleeping in the Castro district ... that's when I met this officer called Big Red ... he was always in the Castro district ... right on the corner there, I was sitting on the steps. What he does is, everybody's sitting on the steps, I'm not by myself, he was fingering me out and telling me, 'You know better. Next time I catch you I'm going to give you a ticket.' And he's been doing it ever since.

Q: And is he in this neighbourhood now?

A: Yeah, in the Tenderloin.

Q: So every time he sees you he picks you up?

A: Yeah, yeah, wherever I sit, I'm out of bounds, I'm trespassing.

Q: And there's no particular reason? He's just got it in for you?

A: No, no particular reason. I've never said anything out of place. I've never disrespected him, but you can't never win. You know that's a no-win situation. Why make it hard for yourself?

Q: And it's just this one guy's got it in for you?

A: This one guy.

Q: Have you had an opportunity to ask him why?

A: Yup.

Q: And what did he say?

A: 'You know better.' That's it.

Whereas police officers in some jurisdictions rely on local ordinances or health codes as tools to 'control' the homeless citizen, in the United Kingdom police often resort to the catch-all offence of 'breach of the peace' to legitimize harassing and arresting individuals. In Scotland,

homeless citizens and community-service providers alike speak dispar-
agingly of the use of this offence to arrest people for short periods of
time. In the following exchange from an interview with a homeless male
shelter user in Edinburgh, he describes the use of 'breach of the peace'
to harass homeless residents who are seen as being too visible near the
new Parliament building:

A: The police, anybody, they just glance at you and if they don't like you and
   the way you look, if you're dirty in any way, they'll stop you and check
   you. There is lots of little Hitlers running around. They'll nick you as soon
   as look at you. If you give them any sort of abuse, they'll give you breach
   of the peace.
Q: Is there a lot of victimization by police officers?
A: I would say so, because Edinburgh is the capital of Scotland … Parliament
   is 100 yards that way … I think the Scottish government, as it's now called,
   tried to move all the homeless out of the city centre and brush it out of the
   carpet.
Q: So do people get picked up or beat up and then dropped off?
A: No, they don't do that anymore. What they do is they will pick you up
   and take you to St Leonard's and release you at strange times. They will
   pick you up, and take you down the road, and let you go at some
   ridiculous times. They will just hold you and then release you.

Despite receiving various forms of cultural and other awareness
training, individual officers are not immune to various forms of discriminatory attitudes, which can result in harassing behaviour towards
racial, ethnic, queer, and other minority groups. This fact was made
patently clear to me while conducting interviews with members of the
GLBT community in San Francisco. Despite San Francisco's much vaunted
liberal attitudes towards sexual minorities, some of the transgendered
women I interviewed noted experiences of harassment by police. One
woman had received verbal abuse on multiple occasions from police
officers. As she explains, 'they tend to disrespect and know the girls are
men. I don't think it's their job to have to put it out there like that.
"Mister, get off the street" and things like that.'
    For some homeless men and women, previous negative experiences
with police include episodes of physical abuse (Novac et al. 2007;
Waccholz 2005). In Toronto, a male shelter resident advises that 'the cops
are well known for taking people from shelters to this place called
"Charity Beach" where they beat them. I've known people who've been

Photograph 3.3 Poster for an anti-police rally (Vancouver)

taken there' (Huey and Quirouette 2009: 18). A service provider in the same city claims that he had 'witnessed police brutally beat clients,' whereas another shelter worker references a case where a client had been 'nearly beaten to death by the police' (ibid.). In Vancouver, a homeless male claims that his 'head was stomped, my nose was broken. I got two teeth kicked out by the Vancouver police' (Huey and Quirouette 2009: 37).

Not surprisingly, violent, abusive, and/or discriminatory treatment by police leads to increased distrust of police and the development of negative attitudes that manifest in an unwillingness to come forward with reports of victimization (Wingert et al. 2005; Mayock and O'Sullivan 2005). These results are easy to discern in the words and actions of homeless citizens. A man in San Francisco burst out laughing at the idea of reporting victimization to the police: 'The cops are so bad that it's like no one gets pushed so far that they want to tell the cops. That's the absolute worst. You could hire someone with a baseball bat, they're much cheaper [laughing]. It's like without any of the difficulty of putting your name on paper and stuff. They're awful [referring to the police]. And the cops are going to beat you too. Nobody wants to talk to the cops.' In some jurisdictions, relations between police and some local residents have grown sufficiently antagonistic that activist groups have started local 'cop watch' programs aimed at documenting and preventing incidents of harassment and/or police abuse (Huey, Walby, and Doyle 2006).

Status Issues

Q: If you were assaulted, would you tell a cop?
A1: [laughing] We can't find them! We can't find them!
A2: [laughing] That's funny, that's funny. They're never there when I need
   them! They're only there to bust my ass. That's the only time they're there!
                                                  – Two homeless men, San Francisco

The streets contain communities that are composed of those who are seen by the police and public alike as criminals, deviants, outlaws, and sinners – that is, as morally tainted and potentially dangerous. Awareness of how they are perceived directly influences attitudes towards reporting victimization by homeless citizens. For instance, in response to a question as to whether anyone in the Tenderloin would feel comfortable reporting a crime to police, a male shelter resident responds bitterly, 'Why? It's not like they're going to scour the town because one junkie ripped another junkie off' (Huey and Kemple 2007: 2316). In telling me of an incident in which he had had a knife pulled on him in sight of a police car, a street drinker in Edinburgh explains that he decided to walk away from the incident rather than reporting it because he was of the view that the police saw it and chose not to act. For him, in the mind of the police officer, he was 'just another drunken homeless person' (Huey

2007: 79). Other researchers have similarly found that the issue of status is tied to the belief shared by many homeless citizens that the police will not see them as credible victims. In London, S. Ballintyne (1999) found that 60 per cent of homeless people surveyed believed that they would not be taken seriously if they reported an offence to police. When asked why she didn't report her victimization to police, a homeless woman in Florida interviewed by J. Jasinski et al. (2010: 118) summed up the views of many of the people I've encountered over the years: 'Because I was homeless and the police don't care about homeless people … that's why I don't trust them.'

Fears of homeless victims that their status reduces their credibility in the eyes of police are not always unfounded, as is made clear in many stories related in interviews. In the following exchange, a homeless male resident of Toronto discusses his experience of an assault that was dismissed by attending officers:

A: I was badly beaten and this was at the Concourse for Cumberland Terrace. As a matter of fact, I'll show you. There is a mark here on my wrist, from the cuffs. I attempted to press charges, but that went nowhere with the cops.

Q: OK. Can you talk more about that?

A: Well, they regarded it as a joke. The bastard called the cops because I'm to be removed from the premises. So, eventually the cop gets there and I protest it long and loud. And the cop stands beside and says, 'Oh. You've been framed?' It was all bull. As for the guy, he was … the irony is I actually served in the naval reserve, so I know discipline. This guy was a goof Sergeant that Hollywood would promote. He was making remarks about how it was all society's fault. I told him I had university education and that sort of took him aback.

Q: So, he didn't take you seriously and was not on your side?

A: Yeah, the cop didn't.

In speaking of why he would not report victimization, a man in Toronto states, 'Cops are so quick to judge. Say you're in an alley and you've been victimized, so you go to the cops and the cops go, "What were you doing in the alley? Were you smoking crack?" This same individual subsequently notes that he has 'a lot of working girls as friends and it's surprising how often I've had them say to me, "I asked for my money and the guy almost choked me to death."' He adds, 'I don't even bother saying, "Why don't you go to the police?"' because the women are engaged in illegal activities and so their stories wouldn't be seen as credible. Service providers make similar claims. In Toronto, a woman who works with sex workers says of her clients that 'the police don't treat them with respect, and so they are afraid to disclose anything' (Huey and Quirouette 2009: 21). Another service provider cynically asks, 'Who is gonna believe a prostitute on crack?'

Those with addictions or issues related to mental illness feel particularly vulnerable to police disbelief. A male shelter user in Edinburgh tells the story of a homeless female friend who was being physically abused by a male partner. When asked if she would be comfortable reporting it to the police, he replies, 'She'd do it now. But then … she was on smack' and would therefore not have been treated as a credible victim. In some situations, their drug use and the role that it played in increasing their exposure to victimization causes some homeless citizens to blame themselves for the offence and to regard police as likely to do the same (Jasinski et al. 2010). A Vancouver man illustrates what he thinks the attitude of police is towards victimized drug users: 'Most cops down there, "You know, is it over drugs?" "Yeah." "That's your problem, you shouldn't do drugs."' In relation to mental illness, a service provider who works with mentally ill clients in Vancouver offers the story of a client who was dissuaded from going to the police over an item she believed to have been stolen. The woman was concerned that, once police learned of her psychiatric condition, they would not find her story credible. The service worker concludes that, when it comes to reporting crime, 'mental illness is a huge barrier to your credibility.' Police acknowledge this fact: 'We do know that there are problems with sexual assaults that go unreported,' a police supervisor in Toronto notes. The fact that many victims are homeless and have substance abuse and/ or mental health issues represent huge barriers because 'they think people will not believe them.'

Status also operates as a barrier to crime reporting in other ways. In many jurisdictions, as noted earlier, those who are homeless are routinely ticketed for a variety of status offences, and these tickets often lead to unpaid fines and outstanding warrants. Oftentimes victims have a prior history of offending (Borchard 2005; Pain and Francis 2004) and this history – whether it be for unpaid tickets or an armed assault – also plays a role in how some feel they will be treated by police. In the words of one homeless male in Toronto, 'most of the time when you've had contacts with the police, you're in trouble. So, you want to have as little contact with the police as you can.' When police respond to a call, they check the victim's name. Should they discover an outstanding warrant, police officers are duty-bound to execute it; therefore, victims are often afraid to come forward for fear that they will be arrested. A service provider put his clients' concerns as follows: 'If they were to report, they might wonder what would come of this process. Would they be [treated as] a victim?' (Huey and Quirouette 2009: 22). Police officers acknowledge that this is a problem: 'Many of the women down here have warrants and they get sexually assaulted and they're not going to phone it in. That's a huge barrier' (ibid.: 22). Although officers frequently acknowledge that warrant checking is a significant barrier to reporting for homeless victims, police officers are generally loathe to suspend the warrant-checking process or exercise discretion for minor offences (Huey and Quirouette 2009).

In some cases, homeless victims worry that, even without an outstanding warrant for their arrest, they might find themselves in trouble with police because they have been sleeping rough or consuming drugs. The experience of a male shelter user interviewed in Edinburgh suggests that fear of arrest for status offences can be a valid concern:

A: I was beat up right before I came in here. I was kicked up and down the
   street by a gang of lads who had just come out of the pub. I was sleeping
   in a doorway. Police came and they arrested me.
Q: For what?
A: For vagrancy.

Cultural Issues

Q: So some tourist stabs you in the throat, you still would not call the cops?
A: No. I could be lying there on a hospital bed and because of the beliefs that
   I have stuck to all these years, being a grass or whatever, I still wouldn't.
                                                    – Homeless male, Edinburgh

Street-based communities have cultural values and beliefs that are often distinct from – and sometimes oppositional to – those found within the larger mainstream society. Opposition is a result of feelings of social alienation that leads to the adoption of a normative system known as the 'code of the street' (Anderson 1999). The cultural beliefs and values contained within the 'code of the street' structure the social hierarchy within street-based communities, as well as shaping attitudes and interactions within those communities. Toughness, independence, and a willingness to use violence are seen as socially desirable traits that lead to social success and the ability to protect one's self in an often chaotic space (ibid.). Any sign of mental or physical weakness is not only disdained but can invite predation (Huey and Quirouette 2010). If one is victimized, the proscribed response is to 'deal with it' through retaliation or by simply letting the incident go.[3] What one is not supposed to do is to rely on outsiders – particularly the police – for support. Indeed, a central dictum of the code is the prohibition against informing authorities about criminal or other activities in one's community,[4] a practice variously known as snitching, ratting, and grassing (Akerstrom 1988; Evans, Fraser, and Walklate 1996). Thus, contacting the police marks a clear sign of individual weakness and is viewed as a betrayal of one's community. This prohibition is so entrenched within the thinking of some individuals that they will not even consider reporting offences committed against them by strangers from outside their community, as the following excerpt from an interview with two homeless Edinburgh men makes clear:

Q: If it is not a member of your community, if it's some tourist? Does it only
   count as grassing if it's someone you know?
A1: Yes and no. Yes because there isn't going to be any repercussions, but at
   the same time, it's going to be in the back of your mind, 'I've been a grass
   eh …'
Q: But he stabbed you!
A1: Yeah.
A2: It's sad.
A1: It's a hell of a world, isn't it?
A2: See, I know a guy who got stabbed in the eye and he never grassed.
Q: So you still say that grassing is wrong, no matter what?
A1: Yeah, I have never grassed. I am not a grass.

Being publicly identified as a rat, 'narc,' snitch, or grass can result in threats, harassment, and physical violence, including beatings and stabbings. A man in San Francisco says of ratting, 'Oh yeah, that's dangerous. That's really dangerous. You get nailed as a snitch … that's bad.' When asked why so few homeless people report victimization to police, a shelter resident in Toronto states that the result would be, 'You're in an alley somewhere bleeding to death' (Huey and Quirouette 2010: 286). A man in Toronto explains, 'You don't want to get known as someone who is ratting out their friends. Usually, if you do, you end up in worse trouble afterwards, like, repercussions. You get ostracized and victimized by other friends because you ratted' (Huey and Quirouette 2010: 286). For such reasons, a woman in Vancouver states, 'I'm not gonna rat on anyone. I'm scared of the consequences' (ibid.: 286). A man in Edinburgh succinctly sums up the potential consequences of snitching: 'Basically, if you grass, your life' (Huey 2008: 213). In speaking of the problems he faced having homeless victims and witnesses come forward, a police officer in Toronto says, 'They are honestly afraid.' He then went on to discuss a past experience to illustrate the extent to which fear of retaliation plays a role in individuals not coming forward with evidence: 'I mean we have had homicides in and around shelters. I had one where a homeless guy that everybody was afraid of, he murdered a guy with a brick. And I investigated the same guy for really a terrible assault, like an aggravated assault. These are the guys that everybody knows, and they are all afraid of them.' A significant part of the problem is that homeless communities are small and services are few and concentrated, and thus, in the words of one service provider, 'they have to go out there and live with that person.'

To be clear, 'the homeless' are not a homogeneous population but rather communities of individuals of varying status and with different beliefs and experiences. Some individuals will temporarily join the ranks of those who are homeless and then make the transition back into mainstream society. Others will become homeless but consciously choose to eschew local values and beliefs. And still others are born into 'street families' or are socialized into street values and come to adopt them. Thus, whereas those who are 'street entrenched' are frequently willing to uphold the 'snitching code' (or at least to be seen doing so), many others continue to espouse the values of the dominant society, including holding positive attitudes towards the reporting of crime. For individuals who number among the latter, the cultural prohibition has little meaning; it is simply not a part of the cultural belief system they ascribe to. For example, an interviewee in Toronto refers to the cultural prohibition against informing as 'this whole garbage called "ratting."' In response to a question as to whether he would be concerned with acquiring a reputation as a 'rat' for reporting victimization, another individual in Toronto states, 'No, I live by my own rules.'

Nor are all cultural barriers to reporting the result of adaption to the ethos embodied in the 'code of the street.' We live in increasingly multicultural societies and many of our cities and towns are ethnically diverse. In some cases, victims will opt not to come forward because the type of offence committed against them is seen as 'normal' or acceptable within their former communities. Attitudes towards intimate partner violence offer a perfect illustration of this dynamic. A service provider in Edinburgh says of some of the women she counsels: 'I don't think they would dare to actually use anything to report abuse.' In Edinburgh, a Romanian woman became homeless in Scotland when she fled an abusive husband. When asked if she would ever report the husband, who is also in Scotland, she emphatically says no, that her preferred response is to escape to another city to get away from him.

Also among recent immigrants are those who come from countries where police systems are corrupt, rights are frequently infringed with impunity, and the law offers few, if any, protections. As a service provider in Toronto explains of some of the immigrant groups he works with, 'they've come here because their families were in danger – intimidated by the police, being kidnapped and ransomed. Then they come to a country where some of that has to heal, so they can rebuild trust with authority.' This problem is also one that police are aware of. 'A lot of them come from countries where there is no trust with the police,' an officer in Toronto notes. The question, he suggests, is 'how could policing agencies rebuild trust so that immigrant groups would see the police as a resource rather than as a source of oppression?' This is a worthwhile question, albeit one that needs to be considered in relation to homeless citizenry as a whole.

Security?

Nobody wants to come forward. They do not want to deal with the system. They have been through the system and they do not want to go through the system again. That is why a lot of them do not bother reporting or they do not think that we give a shit about them.

– Police officer, Toronto

In this chapter I have focused on the police as the primary providers of public security for citizens. What the preceding discussion documents is that, while there are some citizens who do consider the police a potential source of security, many others do not. For those within this latter group, we find that there are often three interrelated factors that disproportionately affect their attitudes towards police and police reporting. The first of these, and the most obvious, is the often antagonistic relations between police and homeless citizens. While this is not found to be universally the case, it is often more common in some communities to find homeless citizens who see the police more as a source of oppression than as a public service from which they can derive benefits. Police practices such as moving people along and conducting illegal stops and searches, as well as harassment and abuse, contribute to an environment in which the homeless citizen sees the police as the enemy and respond accordingly. Among those responses is the withdrawal of trust, which manifests in victims and witnesses who are unwilling to come forward and report to an institution they have little faith in. As a reactive institution whose mandate is served largely through the willingness of citizens to mobilize their services, police often find homeless communities impenetrable sites and must rely on informers or community agents for the little information they can glean on local crimes (Huey 2008).

In *Crime in an Insecure World*, Richard Ericson (2007: 205) notes a central problematic in relation to policing at the margins: the nature of their work requires officers to make split-second judgments as to the nature of an incident and its participants, allocate blame, and respond accordingly. When decisions are made as to how to situate people in relation to that incident, police employ status cues as an useful heuristic (Bittner 1990). Not being immune from the prejudices that most of us face, it is the homeless citizen who frequently emerges as less than credible in the eyes of the police. The frequent result is that homeless victims often feel disillusioned by the criminal justice system and revictimized by its processes, leading to what one police officer in Toronto correctly notes is a 'lack of faith in society.' All of this, in turn, contributes to the chronic insecurity that is a chief characteristic of life on the streets.

A further significant barrier to police mobilization on crime issues is the existence of a cultural code that contains an actively enforced prohibition against informing to the police. While some exceptions to this prohibition are said to be culturally acceptable, in actual practice few are (Huey 2010). Victims can therefore easily find themselves not only branded as a 'grass,' 'rat,' or 'snitch' but the subject of harassment and/or physical violence from the offender, his or her friends, or other members of the local community. Fear of retaliation contributes further to insecurity.

Under traditional views of citizenship, the state is obligated to provide forms of public security through the creation of laws enforced through the mechanisms of the criminal justice system. Stripping away all other positive and negative rights that have evolved over time, we are left with this obligation as the basis of the social contract. It is worth noting that this is a bargain that has not been superseded by the introduction of aspects of U.S. neo-liberal ideology and the push to make citizens more responsible for their own lives. Indeed, although its reach has become attenuated and its ability to provide services substantially weakened in parts, the state – and the public police as its law-enforcement arm – remains the primary guarantor of security for most citizens. At present, this is not unequivocally true for all citizens, as the discussion above makes evident. When it comes to the matter of physical security for the homeless citizen, the state is a terribly imperfect source. As a result, the state is also inadequate to the task of fostering ontological security among homeless citizens. Thus, homeless individuals have been forced to develop their own security strategies and modes of protection. Although frequently deemed better than relying on the state for security, as we shall see, these adaptations are not without their own significant limitations.

4 Self-Protection Strategies

I feel safe no matter where I am. I can look after myself.

– Homeless male, Toronto

Walking through the DTES with a colleague one afternoon, I noticed a young woman on a corner, waiting for a light. I gave her a quick glance and continued scanning the street. Apparently, my female colleague also spared her a glance, because the woman started yelling, 'What are you looking at, bitch?' This was followed by, 'Who the fuck do you think you are? You want me to fuck you up?' The light changed and we crossed the street, with the incensed woman trailing after us, continuing a barrage of haranguing. My colleague looked down and tried to avoid the woman's gaze, but I caught it and held her eyes for a second. Then, very sweetly, I asked, 'Excuse me. Could you please help us? We're trying to find the Salvation Army mission and we're about ready to give up.' Within mere moments the woman who had threatened to 'fuck up' my colleague became friendly and helpful, as we stood there effusively thanking her for giving us directions.

As this story illustrates, successful adaptation to life on the streets requires the cultivation of various survival skills, including being conscious of one's posture and demeanour and learning to conform both to fit into a given environment. The woman we encountered clearly thought that my colleague – an outsider – was negatively judging her. By posing as people who were lost and growing frustrated trying to find a location, we offered a viable alternative explanation for any negative glances the woman might have perceived. In essence, we were employing 'street smarts' as a way to de-escalate the situation and avoid a potential physical altercation.

Since most homeless citizens do not have the means to access the private security market and are either unable or unwilling to rely on the public police for reasons discussed in the previous chapter, they are forced into becoming more or less responsible for their own personal security. To look after their individual security on the streets, they must quickly learn a variety of techniques for increasing personal safety, including the development of street smarts. I note with no little irony that advocates for true market economies hold up as a workable ideal the notion of a populace that is no longer dependent on state services but has instead been responsibilized into becoming educated, reflexive managers of their own personal risks (Ericson, Barry, and Doyle 2000; O'Malley and Palmer 1996; O'Malley 1992). Employing the logic of this form of neo-liberal discourse, then, we could say that through the failures of the state, the homeless citizen has been 'empowered' to look after his or her own security interests. Indeed, taking this notion further, and becoming even more ironic in the process, we could even argue that when it comes to security and management of personal risk, the homeless individual represents the neo-liberal ideal of a responsibilized citizen.

Street Smarts

Someone who does have street smarts knows what to do.

– Homeless woman, Toronto

Perhaps foremost among survival necessities is the acquisition of 'street smarts,' the colloquial term for forms of experiential knowledge acquired within local street-based cultures and used prescriptively to guide individual behaviour. As an example, newcomers must learn to be aware on the streets and to 'read' the behaviour of others, scanning for signs of potential threats (Mayock and O'Sullivan 2007). For instance, a homeless woman in Montreal says of being out on the street:

A: You just gotta watch out, what you're doing.
Q: And so when you say watching what you're doing, are you like scanning the street?
A: Yeah.

A woman in Vancouver watches people closely and decides whom she will talk to based on the 'vibe' she receives from them – that is, a reading of their postures and demeanour – and the extent to which she feels comfortable in their presence. 'I don't talk to people,' she says, 'unless I get that vibe.' For others, awareness is viewed as 'staying on the defensive,' as illustrated by the comments of a woman in Montreal: 'When you're out the street you're safe [if] you stay only on the defensive.' Another woman, interviewed in a homeless day centre in Ottawa, describes her self-protective awareness of what is happening in the streets as a 'sixth sense':

A: I have a sixth sense. I can tell if something's not right I'll just sort of avoid the situation, like walk around it sort of thing.
Q: So, like duck down the block or ...?
A: No, not really. If I see something fishy on my side of the street, I'll just like cross the street or something.

Street smarts encompass two different forms of knowledge: knowledge that is learned first-hand through personal observation and experience; and the collective wisdom of community members' experiences, transmitted through the act of storytelling.

Lessons drawn from personal experience are used to develop individual rules or prescriptions embodying personal security strategies intended to minimize risk. For example, a homeless woman in Montreal who engages in sex work says that to stay safe she has learned not to go into 'strange cars' because 'I have had a lot of bad experiences in cars, and so I have learned not to go back in them, not to get into that situation.' Substance use often places individuals in vulnerable positions, and it is not uncommon to hear of women, the elderly, or young people being sexually assaulted when intoxicated. In fact, plying individuals with drugs and alcohol in order to sexually abuse or assault them is a well-known predatory strategy. One offender in Edinburgh was particularly known throughout the community for finding vulnerably elderly women, plying them with too much alcohol, and raping them once they had passed out (Huey 2007). To prevent such victimization, a woman in Montreal has learned to watch her alcohol intake around strange males because if one 'gets too drunk and you don't know what you're doing and the guy will force sex on you.' Another woman from the same shelter says that exposure to the streets has taught her that staying safe means, 'You learn to bite before you get bit.'

In their article 'Culture as Figurative Action,' C. Shearing and R. Ericson (1991) demonstrate how the police occupational subculture is one in which lessons drawn from experience not only guide individual action but also come to form part of the 'recipe rules' of policing – that is, the informally adopted stratagems to be employed in a given situation. These 'informal cookbook rules' are transmitted to new officers via stories (ibid.: 489). The employment of storytelling as a means of transmitting experiential knowledge is not limited to the police; rather, we can also find its use among street-based cultures. When these stories are analysed, they are seen to contain knowledge that the speaker has acquired about how to stay safe (either directly or through others) and is now attempting to pass along. For example, a man in Toronto weaves an illustrative story into an explanation of how one chooses which shelters are safer to stay at and why:

> So, at [Shelter X] there was an ex-street guy who was incorporated into their staff. So, this guy – Indian, drunk, and prone to violence – decided he didn't like what this non-Indian guy did. So, he decided to rough him up. And, the staff, they allowed this in full view. And this is in no means an isolated case. There is the religious aspect, and a lot of these guys don't like religion. So, the worst of the worst will tend to stay away. What you have here [indicating the shelter where the interview was held] is a stratified nuance, is the best of the worst. They are better than what you will find in these other places. Some of them are absolutely notorious. [Shelter Y] is this shelter in the East End. I'm sure you've heard of [Shelter Z]? I hear you sleep with your shoes on.

While some of this man's knowledge of shelters and their relative safety has been learned first-hand, the last sentence clearly indicates that he has also been the recipient of some of the local collective wisdom. A story told by a woman in Vancouver illustrates not only a technique for disabling an opponent but the culturally appropriate response to potential victimization (discussed in more detail in the next section):

> I walk down here today and I have my Walkman here. These are different headphones. A friend of mine gave them to me because she ripped it. This girl comes in. I guess she was a hooker. She thought I was talking to her but I wasn't talking to her. She goes, 'You got my CD player.' I go, 'What are you doing?' I go like this and she tripped. Phil taught me how to do that. Went around her leg here, and the other one around the other leg. I go,

'Don't ever do that shit again.' She goes, 'Wait a minute, I know that move.' She goes, 'You know a guy named Phil?' I go, 'That's my boyfriend, why? I'm on my way down to see him.' She goes, 'Oh, I guess you can say hi to him.' I go, 'I guess you didn't get my player. Nice try. What do you think? I'm a newcomer around this area? No, I'm an oldie,' and I kept walking.

A common rule within homeless communities is 'keep your mouth shut and your eyes open' because 'the less you know the safer you are' (Hatty, David, and Burke 1999: 179). The importance of this rule is demonstrated through the following story told by a homeless male in Toronto:

> Well, friends, basically this happened maybe about two and half weeks ago. A friend came to me and tried to muscle me for some money for some drugs. As a friend to a friend, I knew he had enough and he had ... he was past his limit. You can only get so high so much, and I'm sitting at thirty-four days clean and I said, 'Don't put that on me. I told you I don't want that on me at this time in my life. I'm trying to do good for me and for myself.' And he said, 'I heard you can get a hold of something.' I didn't respond to him, so he sent somebody down to try to burn me out of my place. I came out of my place and I got piped down with two-foot pipes ... because I wouldn't, basically, give them what they wanted. And this is a friend I've known for like five years. A so-called friend, let's say. Now, for me to go to the police for something like that, that's the last thing I want to do. The reason I don't go to the police is because you'll black mark yourself, for one. Like a rat, the number one reason. That means you're not safe.

A group that is particularly vulnerable to predation on the streets is homeless youth. Among the various factors that play a role in increasing their risk to victimization is a lack of streets smarts. As R. Anderson (1996: 371) suggests, few arrive on the streets with sufficient smarts to be immediately successful at adapting to street life, and the process of learning how to be street smart can involve 'a steep learning curve, sometimes requiring years of experience.' A young man in Vancouver, who had trusted the wrong people and was victimized by them, examines his own learning curve and the effect of not being streetwise during his early days of homelessness: 'Y'know, streetwise people, they know what they're doing and they the leech all the money they can out of people. I'm streetwise, but not as streetwise as most of these people here ... I'll never be that naive again. I've had it happened to me too many times. I'm more intelligent now. But before ...'

Having street smarts is, unfortunately, not an automatic guarantee of safety. As Anderson (1996) notes, the personal security of a homeless person can easily be jeopardized as a consequence of the individual choosing to ignore acquired street knowledge. Certain factors – including addiction or the need for food or shelter – make such decisions more likely. The following story is told by a Vancouver woman, whose sister was one of the victims of serial killer Willie Pickton. This story illustrates the degree of desperation that can drive someone to knowingly take a significant safety risk:

> Now, I'll tell you what happened to my sister … She's living at the hotel. She and her friend [name omitted[1]] had been out to the pig farm a couple of times. They were treated really well the times that they were out there together. They were to entertain the men and they also had them to do porn movies, and toward the end of the night they sort of pretended to kill them a couple of times. Pretended to. They paid them really well and sent them back home. All the girls that lived at the Empress that had been out there two times, my sister started to notice they weren't coming back the third time. She said to [her friend], 'Don't go back out there. We've been out twice, don't go back out.' My sister was intending not to go back out there, but what happened is that the next time a girl had been out there twice and was hard up for her drug of choice, heroin, this woman, Tina,[2] who knew all the girls at the hotel and knew they'd been out there before. Next time she was hard up for a drug, the girl would get a knock at the door and say, 'Willie's here for you.' This happened to my sister … My sister knew what it meant, that she wouldn't come back. But she was so hard up for that heroin that she thought she could sweet talk him out of it.

According to the woman, her sister met Pickton in an alleyway behind her SRO hotel and was physically assaulted and nearly kidnapped before she was able to bluff the killer into releasing her.[3] As this story makes evident, not having or applying street smarts can have potentially fatal consequences.

Being 'Tough'

I settle my own problems, my own way.

– Homeless male, Vancouver

In his ethnography of life in the inner-city of Philadelphia, E. Anderson (1999) details the many ways in which the young males he studied use demonstrations of toughness and overt violence as means of preventing their own victimization. Macho performances of toughness are also found within homeless communities, where individuals similarly seek to build a reputation for violence in order to deter potential victimizers. Indeed, a service provider in Edinburgh remarks that incidents in her shelter are often the result of fighting because 'some kid wants respect, they're building respect.' The tough persona is neatly encapsulated in the words of a homeless man interviewed in Toronto: 'Basically, I'm not the one that's going to be out there being punked everyday, getting robbed. So if somebody comes robbing me I'm telling you I'm beating your ass. Straight up, that's the way it goes. You try to rob me, I'm beating your ass, straight up.' 'A lot of people know me around here and they know that I can fight,' another homeless male in Toronto says, adding, 'So people don't fuck with me.' When it comes to projecting toughness as a defensive strategy, size clearly helps: 'I'm a large guy, right?' still another man in Toronto notes. 'Not too many people will bother me. They're scared that I might retaliate and hurt them pretty quick.'

The masculinist values embodied within local homeless cultures also shape how many of the women within these communities view their security options. Those who can fight, and are willing to do so, will use violence as a means of establishing a tough reputation, as the following excerpt from an interview with a woman in Ottawa demonstrates:

A: Basically like I mean, especially around here it's like, well, don't screw with her, cause basically she'll screw you up. I don't know, it must be an air I have put out that I don't realize.
Q: Have you developed a rep?
A: Oh yeah [laughs].
Q: Okay, okay. There you go.
A: Oh yeah, don't fuck with her, she's a bitch, you don't want to get on her bad side, don't give her bad looks. It's hard to wind down that type of thing. I have a temper and I don't let it show and you do not want to get me pissed off cause when I do get pissed off it's like 'look out' [laughs]. So and a lot of people know that.

When asked about how she stays safe on the streets in Ottawa, a woman who has been homeless for over twenty years replies, 'I act tough and I am not really that tough, really, but just so the image like it scares people off and that seems to work' (Huey and Berndt 2008: 188). In describing how she acts similarly tough to protect herself, a woman in Montreal responds, 'I get rude sometimes and violent maybe.'

While conducting interviews with homeless women in Edinburgh and San Francisco in 2003, I became aware of the fact that the 'tough guise' adopted by many of the women I met extended beyond acts of aggression or tough speech to how they carried themselves (erect posture, assertive eye contact), how they pitched their voices (low and deep), and how they dressed (baggy T-shirts, jeans, golf shirts, and jean jackets[4]). Oftentimes initial impressions of women as 'tough' gave way and, as they relaxed and opened up, their voices and demeanours changed, becoming softer, less harsh or assertive. Several of the women also referenced, often in passing, ways in which they 'act tough' as a self-protective strategy on the streets. From such exchanges, I began to realize the extent to which their initial approach was a performance, one that I term the 'masculinity simulacrum' (Huey and Berndt 2008). In later interviews conducted, I began to explicitly ask female participants whether they consciously performed 'tough masculinity' as a safety strategy to deter potential victimizers and, if so, how they shaped their performance (ibid.). The Ottawa woman mentioned above who said that 'I act tough and I am not really that tough, really, but just so the image like it scares people off and that seems to work,' elaborated on the 'tough guise' she adopts to avoid becoming a crime target:

Q: So, do you change your voice?
A: Yes. It goes deep like a man's voice.
Q: And what about your body?
A: I walk with my arms out, very butchy kind of look.
Q: And do you dress like that sometimes too?
A: Yeah, I don't dress feminine (Huey and Berndt 2008: 188).

In describing such performances, women tend to use words such as 'butch' or 'like a boy,' as do those service providers who work with them. For example, a Montreal shelter worker describes one of her clients in the following terms: 'There is one woman in here, she looks like a butch, but she's not here, she doesn't no longer come here. But you can tell that's a woman who will, she will use that butch style so that she doesn't get anyone around her. Like, she'll push them away, so that they know she's not there for anything.' A woman in the same shelter describes her demeanour on the streets: 'I do, um, you know, do present myself and kind of act a bit like a boy. When I feel safe, um, I will just be myself; I will be my feminine self. But when I feel intimidated, by just anybody walking down the street, I'll go, "I belong here" [her voice deepened, her posture became more erect]' (ibid.: 188). As with the woman just cited, other female respondents acknowledge pressures to hide signs of femininity, which might be viewed as weakness on the streets. 'Sometimes we have to downplay being a woman,' an interviewee in San Francisco states. 'To be tougher than what we seem to be ... A lot of us, we have to get tough like that. So hard core. So, almost manly like, to live out here. We can't be vulnerable. We can't show feelings. We can't show anything. For us women, it's very hard' (ibid.: 189).

Few people are, however, sufficiently tough or sufficiently convincing in their performance as to deter all potential threats, and thus victimization stills happens. In those situations, as part of demonstrating one's toughness and autonomy, the 'code of the street' dictates that retaliation is the appropriate response. The exercise of retaliation is commonly referred to by the umbrella term 'dealing with it,' which incorporates a wide range of responses, from threats and harassment to assault and even murder. In Edinburgh one fellow exemplifies the local cultural attitude towards responding to victimization: 'I just got released from prison on the 24th, and when I went out my house got broken in. I went to the guy's house who had done it, and threw a brick through the window. He bothers me, but I'm not going to phone the police. I'm just going to deal with it myself.' In Toronto, a man advises that it is more common for a victim to gather 'two or three of your friends, and catch [the victimizer] when they are inebriated. You just walk by and step on their fingers' (Huey and Quirouette 2010: 287). So common is the practice of retaliatory violence that one man in Vancouver says that in the DTES 'a lot of justice is street justice ... Myself, I've never been in that situation, but I'm close enough to it and you can go through there any day and see it. Even living in this place, you can hear some pretty wicked horror stories.' In response to the question of whether he would ever report victimization, a man in Toronto replies, 'I'm not sure. Paybacks are a bitch.' A man in Vancouver laughs when asked if he would report victimization to the police: 'Why would I call the cops? I'm going to take care of it myself.' As with willingness to use violence as a pre-emptive or defensive strategy, women are also among those who engage in retaliatory violence. As a homeless female in Toronto explains, when it comes to being victimized, 'a lot of the younger women would rather take care of it themselves ... getting back.'

Conversely, if the ability to successfully demonstrate toughness can potentially avert victimization, then signs of mental or physical weakness, or displays of vulnerability of any kind, can be readily interpreted as opportunities for 'easy pickings.' Thus, one must either 'toughen up' or quickly develop alternative security strategies (Mayock and O'Sullivan 2007). For many, though, 'toughening up' is not a viable option because of physical limitations, age, and/or other issues. Although we tend to think of the streets as a young person's space, there are many elderly homeless within our cities and towns. There are also individuals with debilitating illnesses and disabilities, who are physically unable to defend themselves against stronger, younger offenders, or to engage in retaliation should they be offended against. As an example, an older female shelter resident in Vancouver feels that her arthritis not only makes her vulnerable to victimization but has left her unable to retaliate. 'A few years ago,' she says, 'I would have taken care of it myself. Now I have arthritis and just can't' (Huey and Quirouette 2010: 291). In one notable instance, the age of the victim deterred him from attempting to stop younger members of his community from going after the man who had robbed him: 'I'm telling you right straight out it's going to happen. I even tried to stop it, what's going to come down. The heat's coming down. I tried to stop it already. I told people to back off; I'd look after it myself. I'm sixty-one years old. They said, "Sit down, old man; it's out of your hands now." It's not. I decide what happens. They said, "No sir, we decide. Sit down. It's out of your hands." I don't want it to happen this way. They said, "Too bad old man, sit down. Sit down and take a back seat because now you have no control. Somebody's going to do this, take care of this fellow."'

Using Weapons

Q: How do you take care of yourself?
A: How do I? [laughter]. I usually walk around with a lot of stuff, that's
     for sure.

– Homeless woman, Ottawa

One possible option for deterring would-be victimizers, or to quickly even up a fight, is through the use of weapons (Borchard 2005). Although I tend not to ask study participants whether they carry concealed weapons in order to avoid making them uncomfortable,[5] over the years several homeless citizens have casually mentioned the fact that they use some form of weapon as a means of self-protection. Related research turns up disparate figures. At the lower end of estimates, one group of researchers found that in response to questions about personal security,

14 per cent of the homeless men and 16 per cent of the homeless women interviewed stated that they carry weapons (North, Smith, and Spitznagel 1994). In a study of street youth in Winnipeg, approximately 28 per cent of those surveyed reported routinely carrying weapons for self-defence (Gaetz 2004). Figures were significantly higher in a study of homeless females in New York (Coston 1992). The majority of respondents in two groups – minority females (52 per cent) and non-minority females (66 per cent) – advised that they carry a weapon for protection (ibid.).

Knives are easily obtainable, readily portable, relatively low cost, and sufficiently effective in a fight, thus making them the defensive weapon of choice for many. For example, in discussing this issue, a service provider in Edinburgh estimates that at least four-fifths of his male clients carry concealed knives (Huey 2007). Similarly, a service provider who works with women in Montreal advises that a lot of her clients are 'scared' young women and a 'lot of them have knives with them.' A woman from the same shelter states that she was one of those who used to carry a knife, but no longer does so: 'I had a knife on me and I think I showed it too many times, so I throw him in the garbage, because I don't want to do something. You know, you can't control yourself all the time.'

Although seldom discussed, the presence of guns is not unknown in homeless communities (Borchard 2005). In Edinburgh, a young man contends that 'everybody has a gun.' Subsequently, he makes the interviewer an unusual offer: 'If you want a gun, I can get you a gun.' In Vancouver, a homeless woman is considering acquiring a gun to protect herself from two men who had previously broken into her hotel room: 'I've checked around. It's cheaper for me to buy a gun than it is to get a cell-phone that has 9-1-1 on it. It's cheaper to get a gun. So I may have to protect myself.'

In some communities, pepper spray is illegally sold or traded through the underground economy. A woman in Ottawa advises that 'you wanna buy some pepper spray?' is not an uncommon query. In Montreal, a female shelter user states that she would not use pepper spray because 'it is not allowed,' but that as a defensive weapon 'a can of lime paint is okay.' More often than not, though, defensive weapons are fashioned out of objects close at hand. Another homeless woman in Montreal explains that, when a 'big gang' of youths would harass her or try to take her panhandling spot, 'I was using my syringe to make them go away.' Homeless women have also been reported as carrying bags of rocks as weapons, or chemicals such as ammonia, rubbing alcohol, and/

or hairspray (Coston and Finckenauer 2004). A young alcoholic male in Vancouver's DTES describes using his sherry bottle when he felt threatened in a squat: 'Anything I hear as a gun, man, I lose it. I grab anything. I grabbed that bottle of sherry and I just turned around.'

Avoidance and Target-Hardening Strategies

It is a safety thing. Some of [the homeless] do not want to go to the shelters because they find the criminal activity is higher due to the concentration.

– Police officer, Toronto

The most basic of crime-deterrence strategies used by homeless citizens are among the most commonly employed by individuals in general: avoidance and target-hardening. Avoidance entails staying away from or removing one's self from risky people, places, and situations. Target-hardening strategies are those used to make one's self or property less of an easy and thus attractive target for would-be offenders.

In some cases, individuals tend to craft specific rules – i.e., avoid person X – based on past experience or the collective wisdom that such person represents a potential threat. Indeed, it is usually common knowledge who are the local bullies and troublemakers. In other instances, past experience or collective street wisdom is used to shape more general rules about avoiding particular types or groups of people. For example, the older street drinkers of Edinburgh tend to see younger drug addicts as potential threats. Thus, when asked how they stay safe, many will say that they avoid the addicts, where possible, and congregate instead in established street drinker hang-outs where they feel safer among those within their own social network (Huey 2007).

Self-isolating strategies are also common techniques for reducing one's risk of victimization. 'I don't go near anybody,' a woman from Montreal states. 'I usually watch out for other people' (Huey and Berndt 2008: 189). Another woman from the same city exemplifies this same strategy:

A: I usually stay by myself. I am a loner. I don't go near anybody, I usually watch for other people.
Q: You keep a low profile.
A: Pretty much [laughing].
Q: Is that something you've learned to sort of survive around here?
A: Yup, you just stay out of the way.

Photograph 4.1 Street drinker hangout behind mortuary (Edinburgh)

Elsewhere I have used the term 'invisibility strategy' to describe attempts at self-isolating to limit risk of victimization (Huey and Berndt 2008). I have also noted that this strategy can, ironically, end up increasing not only a person's sense of loneliness but also his or her safety-related fears and anxieties (ibid.). This is particularly the case for one woman, who says that 'in the beginning, it was really hard. I was feeling really alone and, you know, you don't know who you can trust or not' (ibid.: 189).

Whereas self-isolation is a common strategy for increasing one's security, so too is deliberately seeking out well-populated spaces in order to reduce the chances of victimization. 'I would rather be in areas where I am seen, a woman in Montreal says, 'because if I am in areas where I am not seen, that's where it can be dangerous.' When out on the streets, another woman from this same city notes, 'I try to walk in busy area.' This strategy also applies to sleeping. For some rough sleepers, finding well-populated spots to sleep makes sense since increased visibility generated by pedestrian and auto traffic can serve as a potential deterrent for someone who might be intent on robbing them.

Photograph 4.2 Homeless man sleeping (Toronto)

With sexual victimization a very real fear for many homeless women, some heterosexual and bisexual women try to avoid risky situations by presenting themselves as lesbians to males within the community. The rationale for this performance is that women who successfully 'pass' can reject approaching males in a way that permits the latter to 'save face,' a valuable strategy since in other circumstances rejection can lead to harassment and/or physical violence. For example, a woman who self-identifies as heterosexual states that she uses this strategy: 'The one good thing is that since this is San Francisco and we have such a large lesbian population, we just kind of blend in. That's usually a good way to rebound somebody, say, "Oh, I don't do men"' (Huey and Berndt 2008: 190). Similarly, in Montreal, an outreach worker notes that the use of this strategy is common among women in that community: 'Yes, we see that all the time. That's a big thing here. But this is the Village, this is the gay Village so, you know, they blend in' (ibid.: 190). It is important to note, however, that this self-protective technique is not without a significant limitation: it renders individuals potentially vulnerable to the myriad forms of abuse and violence that sexual minorities often face. A woman in Ottawa uses a story to illustrate the point: 'I have seen this one situation, when I was in Toronto, a girl did that. She just didn't want to be bothered by certain guys and she did it one time with this one guy and it totally backfired on her and she got the extreme shit kicked out of her, like I mean, he just didn't like lesbians and so it kind of backfired on her' (Huey and Berndt 2008: 190–1).

Survival may also entail avoiding risky places. Thus, for some homeless citizens, self-isolating can involve sleeping rough rather than risking victimization in shelters where theft, robbery, and assault can be frequent occurrences (Huey 2007; Fitzpatrick and Kennedy 2001). For example, in Edinburgh, rough sleepers often seek out cemetery vaults in the local graveyards because of the privacy and security that being hidden from view affords them (Huey 2007). A Toronto police officer explains the avoidance of shelters in the following terms: 'They'd rather be in the street corner or in a park than in a shelter because that's the norm. There's going to be thievery, there's going to be disease, there's going to be beatings and there's nothing they can do about it. Whereas when they isolate themselves they feel their chances of not getting robbed, not getting beaten up, not contracting some disease is greater.' Another officer in this same city notes the perceived utility of avoiding shelters to reduce risk of victimization: 'A lot of the homeless do not go to the shelters. They would rather stay on the streets because they get robbed or beaten.' Instead of using shelter beds, homeless citizens seek out hidden spots in public and private spaces and sleep under various objects as a means both of protecting themselves from the elements and of obscuring their presence from others. This officer shakes his head when he describes 'guys are sleeping underneath garbage ... [who] have been there for years.'

Mixed-use facilities – that is, facilities that service both male and female clients – are sometimes seen by some homeless women as places to avoid for fear of victimization by males. For instance, a woman residing in a mixed-use shelter in Vancouver repeatedly states that she was unnerved by the experience of being domiciled with strange men: 'It's scary getting on the elevator, getting stopped at the fourth floor some guy gets on. Sometimes these guys get on the elevator and they don't want to push their button. They want to wait till it gets up to your floor. It's, like, why don't you want to get off on your floor before I get to my floor? You've already pushed the button, so he's going up. It's like, what's he planning?' In their study of homeless women in Florida, J. Jasinski et al. (2010) found that several of the women they interviewed had had experiences of being sexually groped or fondled while staying at a shelter. Not surprisingly, then, some women choose to avoid shelters altogether, preferring instead to find alternative spaces to sleep. Youth are also often reluctant to stay in homeless shelters, since most facilities are used by adults. 'Shelters that predominantly house the adult homeless are regarded as a last resort,' J. Hagan and B. McCarthy (1999: 46) note, because 'for most youth, staying on the street is a preferable and, in their view, less dangerous option.' A young homeless female explains why she sees shelters as a last resort: 'I hang out in this shelter and it is full of men. Alcoholics, drug addicts. It is no place for a girl' (Huey and Berndt 2008: 184).

Other places to be avoided include those sites where, owing to economic or other factors, violence is frequent. For example, some homeless citizens try to avoid sites that function as 'drug markets' because turf wars can lead to shootings or stabbings. In Edinburgh in 2003, I was advised by several street drinkers to stay away from Hunter Square, which was known locally as 'the boxing ring' because of the number of violent fights that would break out.

Not only must homeless citizens learn what sites to avoid, they must also 'construct maps' of "safe" (that is, less dangerous) areas within the cityscape' in order to eat, sleep, and socialize safely (Wardhaugh 2000: 96). The following quote from an interview with a man in Toronto illustrates this type of 'mapping': 'I stay in this area and I consider it a bit of a safer area than other parts of the city. I've heard of other parts where it is worse. Where the gangs are; East, Regent Park, that's where the gangs are. I have a friend who is a housing agent, and she wanted me to move to Jane and Wilson. And just … the name scared me. Jane. It's just not safe. I had friends move out of that area, and they told me it just wasn't safe for a poor little white boy [laughs].' In Vancouver, a homeless male living in the city's downtown core says that the map of safety that he has constructed for himself does not include the neighbourhood of the DTES, which he has cast as an unsafe space: 'I avoid the area as much as possible. I've walked down there at night and you see guys running after … I've seen groups of guys tackle one guy with cans of mace and anything, they just mob. It's insane.'

For many homeless citizens, avoidance of potential threats is not always possible. Further, one cannot remain awake and vigilant at all times. Thus, target-hardening strategies to reduce one's attractiveness as a potential victim are required. Such strategies aim to increase both personal security and the security of one's possessions. Since theft is a rampant crime problem within homeless communities, it is not uncommon for individuals to find hiding spots for their possessions or to turn them over to the safekeeping of others (such as trusted service providers). The elderly homeless man described in this book's Introduction, who was routinely robbed of his benefit cheque money, began to turn his funds over to a trusted friend who doled out his money to him as needed, thus making him less of a target for predators.

Various tactics are also used to avoid robberies or being 'rolled' while asleep or passed out. On days when benefit cheques are distributed, some individuals develop varied routines for cashing their cheques, doing so a day or several days after they've been handed out. Daylight increases opportunities for natural surveillance, thus reducing opportunities for victimization. Streetwise homeless citizens thus may also develop sleeping or socializing routines centred on sleeping or being in social spaces only during daylight hours (Dietz and Wright 2005; Brochard 2005). Since shelters are potential sites of victimization, one Montreal woman varies her patterns in order to avoid being targeted: 'If I come to sleep here every night, you take a different room, because sometimes people watch you they see you coming every night, and they know your path and they know your room, and so that's when you can be vulnerable, if they want to attack you.' Others fashion creative uses of space or resources to establish defensive spots where they can sleep. One man in Toronto stated he avoids shelters because of previous experiences of victimization and sleeps rough instead. To reduce his risk on the street, he finds himself 'a secluded corner where I can get my back up against the wall. That way, people have to come up to the front of me to get at me.' Similarly, an enterprising female rough sleeper in Montreal used to sleep on top of a bridge instead of under one. Her rationale was that staying hidden under a bridge might offer greater privacy but would also limit opportunities for natural surveillance if someone decided to try to victimize her. She was aware, however, of the fact that being exposed on the bridge also came with its own risks: 'I was always afraid that somebody comes and just beat me or just push me down the stairs.'

Security?

Nobody takes care of you; you have to take care of yourself.

— Homeless woman, Ottawa

Readers will recognize the fact that many of the security strategies discussed in this chapter are not unique to the homeless citizen. Avoiding dark, empty places or not walking alone at night are well-known basic safety rules. Similarly, most of us were taught as children to avoid strangers and other 'scary people.' And, certainly, staying away from places where one has been victimized in the past, or seen others victimized, would appear to be an example of good sense.

While there is a lot of merit in applying some of the tactics described above, it is important to note that, in terms of physical security, these methods are often highly imperfect. On an abstract level, having rules about avoiding risky people and places seems to make a lot of sense. However, in their application, such rules can be impractical. Homeless citizens require access to resources. In most cities, those resources – food, shelter, medical, sanitary, and other – are highly concentrated in specific geographical areas. Thus, accessing those services always means running the risk of coming into or across spaces with potentially risky people or situations. Avoiding shelters in favour of sleeping rough is another perfect example of how common-sense rules can become problematic. Shelters can be risky places, not only for thefts but also for harassment, intimidation, robbery, and assault. Yet, as I discuss in the next chapter, they are also places that frequently have both natural and electronic surveillance, access rules that limit individual entry to facilities, and staff to provide assistance. Sleeping rough is not without its own problems, including the potential for increased exposure to offenders, thus necessitating the creation of further strategies for limiting risk.

It is also hard to avoid risky situations if one is destitute and the primary means of earning income available are through the illegal economy. One can attempt to reduce individual risk by creating rules related to those activities, but the inherent risks remain.

Further, some of the security techniques noted can actually serve to increase one's risk of victimization. The belief that security, as well as social status, comes from the successful use of violence and other displays of toughness means that individuals within a group will constantly be challenging each other in physical displays of dominance. This fact was referenced above in the comment of the service provider in Edinburgh who said that much of the trouble in her facility comes from young men fighting in their quest for 'respect.' At a certain point, a skilled fighter may appear to be more or less immune from such challenges, and thus more secure, but there is almost always someone with a grudge or desire to topple their status. There is also the fact that age and infirmities eventually catch up with all of us. The sixty-one-year-old man who was robbed and then told by others that they would retaliate on his behalf against his wishes illustrates this point perfectly. Earlier on in the same interview, this man described his own violent past; today he is largely at the mercy of those who are younger, stronger, and tougher. Retaliation is also no permanent solution either. As I discuss in the next chapter, most people within street-based communities rely heavily on social networks for protection. Unless most of the people in the community view the retaliatory act as justified, there is a likelihood that others will step in to engage in their own acts of retaliation on behalf of their friend. Indeed, even those who uphold and engage in this aspect of the 'code of the street' acknowledge that 'paying someone back' often does little more than continue and/or escalate problems within the community (Huey and Quirouette 2010). In short, examination of the belief that one can acquire security through violence proves it to be illusory.

As I noted in the introduction to this chapter, when it comes to issues of personal security, the bulk of homeless citizens, in a rather ironic way, could be said to exemplify the neo-liberal ideal of a responsible citizenry *because they have no other choice*. When it comes to being the 'empowered, responsible individual,' homeless citizens do the best they can to provide for their own security with the limited resources available to them. Chief among these resources is their own ability to devise and execute self-protective strategies. However, with high rates of crime within their communities, and the significant limitations with respect to many of the security strategies employed, it is often not enough to rely solely on oneself to stay safe. In the next chapter I examine how social bonds with others are also used to try to reduce victimization.

5 Security through Others

Everybody looks out for each other.

– Homeless female, Vancouver

The woman sitting next to me looks small and frail. She has been 'home-less forever' on the streets of San Francisco, she says, and her brown face shows the signs of someone who has been ground down by life. She has found me because she heard I was asking about the police and she has something she wants to tell me. Speaking animatedly, she reveals that she is scared. Terrified, actually. Her son had been sexually abused by someone on the streets and had been taken away by the state. She says she has heard stories from other homeless women and is concerned that the police might also abuse him and herself. 'They can easily lie and you're not really safe,' she says. 'When you see them you don't feel safe. No, I never feel safe.' She is no less afraid of the men in her community, many of whom she sees as predators. I ask her, 'How do you protect yourself?' She smiles, 'I pray.'

In turning to a higher power to acquire a sense of security, Alicia[1] is not unique among homeless men and women (Coston 1992). In a perfect world, faith alone would be enough to keep people safe, but in the Tenderloin and other such urban spaces it's not. Instead, safety often requires reliance on others within the community, as Alicia herself demonstrates in subsequently telling me of how she and other homeless women share information and survival tips. So, while Alicia sees her religious faith as keeping her safe, she also relies on her friends. Similarly situated men and women also turn to trusted community-service providers for help or seek out spaces within their local community to eat, socialize, or sleep safely.

The homeless citizen is hardly unique in relying on others in order to enhance individual and collective security. Most of us have friends, family members, or neighbours whom we trust to provide watchful eyes and ears, assist with security problems that arise, offer useful advice, and so on. Through Community Watch and other related programs, some of us may also have larger security ties to our local communities. One major difference lies, however, in the extent to which our reliance on others remains one option among many within our respective individual security portfolios. For many homeless citizens, the choice is radically more limited. Another significant difference can be found in relation to the issue of community as a generative source of security. Over the past two decades, neo-liberal discourse has promoted the notion that all that is required for communities to fulfil a primary role in fostering collective security is capacity building. To that end, various state governments have invested funds and resources into capacity-building initiatives that would allow for a partial transfer of responsibility for community security from the state to local organizations. However, as Steve Herbert (2006) has documented in connection with attempts to develop community policing in urban neighbourhoods in Seattle, poorer communities are often ill-equipped to bear the weight of such projects. As will be seen throughout this chapter in relation to the communities I studied, even the expectation that one might find any sustained sense of security through community may be asking too much.

Friends

I'm not worried about my safety. I still have a lot of people, a lot of friends here.
                                                                – Homeless male, Toronto

A common misconception surrounding homeless citizens is that when encountered in groups they represent some form of threat to other members of society (Alder and Sandor 1989). While conducting fieldwork, I have observed on numerous occasions individual passersby visibly shrinking, walking fast, and manifesting other signs of discomfort around small groups of homeless individuals. While their appearance in groups may cause unease or even invoke fear for some citizens, the reality is that for many homeless individuals staying within a peer group is one of the few means available of protecting one's self from victimization (Vance 1998; Ravenhill 2008). Indeed, individual friends, peer groups, and extended social networks often play significant roles in enhancing individual and collective security within homeless communities. They do so in at least three ways: 1) by fostering dissemination of safety-related information and strategies ('watching out'); 2) by serving as a deterrent to would-be offenders through their presence; and 3) by coming to the aid of threatened or vulnerable group members.

As the example provided by Alicia above demonstrates, one of the major security benefits of being part of a social network is that members 'watch out' for each other. In homeless communities, 'watching out' for each other typically entails a variety of actions centred on alerting friends and peers to any person, place, or thing that is identified as a potential threat, and responding when assistance is required (Coston and Finckenauer 2004). I became aware of this practice when walking through the DTES. I could hear what sounded like hissing from groups of people hanging out on the sidewalks and in the parks. At first I thought they were hissing to express disapproval over my presence, but it was subsequently explained that what I was actually hearing was the word 'six,' street code for 'watch your back, there's a police officer at six o'clock' (Huey 2007). Individuals within street families and friendship networks demonstrate personal and community bonds through 'watching out' for one another, passing along information that helps keep others safe. Indeed, in response to a question as to whether he would ever discuss an incident of victimization with his friends, a homeless male interviewed in Edinburgh states, 'Oh, yes, we talk about everything ... that's the best thing we can do for each other.' A homeless female, who has formed tight bonds with others in her community, says that she and another woman 'kind of look after everybody' in their group, and that when individuals come forward to share, these women pass on information about safety issues and how to respond to them. In her words, 'they'll tell us something happened and we'll say you should go here and this system will work.'

While it is common practice to 'watch out' for one's friends and pass along suitable information about potential threats, such warnings are especially critical for those engaged in high-risk activities. It is not uncommon, for example, for individuals who earn funds through the sex trade to share information with each other and with service providers about 'bad dates.' Sex workers also 'watch out' for each other in other important ways, including working in pairs or serving as spotters and observing what cars their friends and colleagues are getting into. Indeed, the presence of friends and other workers is often one of the only means of reducing a sex worker's risk of victimization (Shannon et al. 2008). As a woman in Montreal explains, they have to 'watch who they're going with.' To stay safe, sex workers need to 'have positive friends and stay with their friends.' Being out of sight of friends and other observers, she adds, means that women could be 'jeopardizing their safety.'

For many people on the streets, their network of friends and acquaintances becomes a form of family (Hagan and McCarthy 1999). In describing the shelter he was staying at, a fellow in Edinburgh refers to it as 'everybody's house,' and his friends there as a 'sort of family.' A young man in Vancouver who has been staying in a temporary squat talks about his 'street brothers' as 'family members.' Similarly, a female resident of a women's shelter states that the women form little groups, with one woman taking on the role of being 'the mommy of the bunch.' The link between survival and strong friendship ties within homeless communities is explained by a service provider in Toronto in the following terms: 'Regardless of how complicated and difficult it is to live with the people who they are living with, there is a very strong sense of community. It's stronger than most of us experience in our lives. They rely on one another for shelter, support, food, information … and you know jeopardizing those relationships is jeopardizing their general safety.'

In some instances, friendships spring up through a sense that one can be secure around the other person. To illustrate, it is a common practice for shelters to turn out clients in the morning, requiring the latter to find safe alternative spaces during the day. At one shelter in Montreal, many of the clients go to a nearby park, which is often populated by both male and female homeless citizens. A service provider at this shelter notes that many of the women she works with often develop routines centred around going to the park at a particular time in order to be around an individual or individuals with whom they feel secure. As she explains: 'Yeah, yeah, cause they cling to certain people. That goes with the park thing around here. They see this person that they see frequently in a park, they'll talk to them and they will feel protected by them. So, that is the same park, the same place, the same time. There goes the routine thing again where they will go and meet that person, and they feel secure with that person, because he hasn't hurt them yet. He hasn't done anything wrong to them and she feels secure. A lot of·them have that.' She later notes that, when clients are asked what they will do during the day or what they have spent their time doing, they frequently reply,

'"Sittin' in the park with so and so" or "I am going to meet so and so in that park at two o'clock and then I will be here at three o'clock."' The service provider adds that, because a particular individual is seen as enhancing her clients' security, women will also say, 'If he goes to the other park I follow him to the other park.'

Hanging out in family groups or travelling with friends also provides individuals with increased security because the presence of others – who are both potential witnesses and responders to an action – frequently serves as a deterrent to would-be offenders. A young woman in Ottawa says that, to avoid being harassed or harmed on the streets, she only goes into public spaces with others: 'I live in a rooming house and there is one other woman in the rooming house besides me, and to avoid getting hurt and stuff like that, when I go out I go with my fiancé or I go with the other girl in the building. I never go anywhere else.' A woman in the DTES who is afraid that she could be the victim of retaliatory violence 'started having my friends walk me around because I got really scared and the cops weren't listening.' 'When we all go out of here,' a resident of a Vancouver women's shelter remarks, 'just for your own personal safety, we go with somebody else … the buddy system is the best system.'

Watching out for each other means being willing to come to the aid of threatened or vulnerable friends. In the streets of Vancouver, homeless youth tend to congregate along the Granville Mall, where they can not only make money through panhandling but also keep an eye on each other. This ethic of care is evidenced in the words of a homeless female adolescent who is protected on the streets by other youth: 'Or if somebody offers you money for sex and stuff and he won't leave you alone, if a couple people that we know – more street kids – they'd be like, "What the hell are you doing?"' (Huey 2007: 9). A fellow in Toronto claims that he has many friends, largely because of his reputation and willingness to come to their aid: 'I got a lot of people that hang with me because they know they're not going to get robbed, they're not going to get stabbed, they're not going to get mistreated. That's why people hang with me like that.' In Edinburgh, street drinkers who pass out are often protected from potential victimization through the actions of friends. One street drinker is routinely assisted by his mates: 'He was that drunk that he can't even walk alone. He just lays down on the sidewalk; he lies on the corner,' a friends notes. 'A lot of people knows him, and everybody that knows him carries him.' With the experiences of this particular street drinker in mind, I asked a homeless female from his area about what

other community members would do if they saw someone harassing or
bullying an older person:

A: They'd say something. Aye. They're not going to let them get away with
   that.
Q: So everybody watches out for each other?
A: Aye. We're all close knit together when we're out on the street together.
   You know what I mean?

The antagonisms between the older street drinkers and the younger
addicts in Edinburgh do not play out among the addict population
itself: younger addicts watch out for older friends and acquaintances.
'The younger crew, they always take care of the older ones,' a female
addict states, adding that such assistance is based on 'respect for each
other.' The willingness to protect vulnerable friends and acquaintances
is also demonstrated in the story of a woman in Toronto:

> A lot of places where I panhandle, there's a lady who was victimized.
> She's so scared to go for a walk by herself … they're banging on the door
> one day and she calls me. I was downstairs. She called the cops. I go, 'Did
> you call the police?' She said, 'Yeah, they said they were on their way like
> two hours ago. The guy's still there, he thinks somebody else lives here. I
> need help.' So I ran upstairs and I had my stick. I go, 'Get away from her
> door.' He goes, 'What'd you say?' I go, 'There ain't nobody there but an
> old lady. She's eighty years old. You're scaring the hell out of her.' He goes,
> 'What are you going to do with that?' I go, 'I'll smack you with it.' He goes,
> 'Yeah right' … I whacked him in the back because he went to kick the door
> again. I hit him.

When someone has been victimized, there is often an expectation that
his or her friends or acquaintances will retaliate. In the following excerpt
from an interview with a homeless male in Toronto, he discusses not
only how he seeks to protect his friends but how such protection encom-
passes retaliatory violence: 'You disrespect me or my family or my
friends then you're not welcome in our neighbourhood … let's say
you're part of my friendship or who I hang with, somebody hurts you
and you bring it to my attention, I'm going to do everything to deal with
it right then and there or by tonight … and you're going to have closure
ten times quicker, a result ten times quicker. Or the payback of whatever
he took because he can't go down and hurt somebody, or let's say

victimize them, when they shouldn't be put in that situation' (Huey and Quirouette 2010: 286–7). For this fellow, retaliation on behalf of his friends is not just about revenge but is rather necessary to prevent further victimization of his 'family': 'If you buckle once, whether it's for five dollars or for five thousand dollars, your name now goes in a pot and now you'll buckle it. People know to find that out. So, that's where I come along … you have security, it won't happen to you again.' This man is hardly alone in believing that friendship entails participating in retaliatory violence. Another individual interviewed in a shelter in Toronto responds to a question about how he would deal with victimization as follows: 'It's sad to say. How many friends do you have in here? That's the thing.' Similarly, an elderly man advises that he doesn't retaliate because he doesn't need to 'do that stuff.' Instead, there are 'enough guys around here that if they saw that happening to me, would come up and say, "Sam,[2] we'll take care of that guy."' Sometimes the nature of the offence might lead to a wider response within the community. For example, a man in Vancouver advises that, 'if a woman gets raped,' which is considered a violation of the street code (Huey and Quirouette 2010), 'she can go get her friend, her dealer, anybody else to go and deal with that person, and I'll pity that person that they find.'

Intimate Partners

I have always had this sort of male blanket around me.

– Homeless woman, Ottawa

One means by which some citizens on the streets acquire increased physical security is through having a tough or intimidating sexual partner (Bourgois et al. 2004; Johnsen, Cloke, and May 2005; Ravenhill (2008). Upon asking a transgendered woman in San Francisco if she had experienced harassment or any other problems from males in the community, she laughed. 'No, because I'm a married woman now and where I go, the daddy's usually not too far behind.' A shelter worker in Montreal, who works with a number of women involved in the sex trade, describes one of her clients as having 'a pimp here and she felt protected by him.' Whereas other women were often afraid to leave the shelter, the service worker says that this client felt that no one could touch her without her permission because of the presence of her pimp, who was also her sexual partner.

It is not only the physical presence of partner that can serve as a deterrent: if he or she has a reputation within the community, then knowledge of that individual's status as a partner can have a similar effect. 'They know me around here,' says the previously cited 'married woman.' 'I've been around here a long time, and they know my husband so ... they don't want to deal with him.' This woman also acknowledges her feelings about the ontological security engendered by having a male partner with a tough reputation in the community: 'I like it because it makes me feel good.'

In discussions with homeless women, several noted that women in particular often seek out male partners not only for companionship but also for physical protection. A long-term female resident of San Francisco's Tenderloin explains this strategy as being most commonly employed by newcomers: 'A lot of women, when they first get out there, they don't know what to do. They're scared. So they get hooked up with some men.' (Huey and Berndt 2008: 187). Similarly, a woman in Toronto says of female newcomers that 'some of them can't cope with Toronto, or a big city. They get taken advantage of.' As a result, she says, 'they think they need a man to look after them.' A woman in Montreal also notes that it is not unusual for scared newcomers to barter sex for security: 'They'll do what it takes; they'll have sex just not to get into any trouble.'

Community Facilities

I won't tolerate inappropriate behaviour; somebody who exhibits that behaviour is challenged immediately and steps are taken.
                                        – Community-service worker, Edinburgh

Community facilities – soup kitchens, day centres, and so on – serve multiple functions within the lives of homeless citizens. For most sites, those functions include being a space of refuge from the violence and other problems the homeless face on the streets. Upon asking the founder of a soup kitchen in Edinburgh about his new facilities, his desire for an environment that fosters feelings of mental and physical well-being is explicit: 'What is central to that is that users feel safe – not just are safe – but that there's a perception of safety. A perception of, that it's almost like a sanctuary in here, and receive a meal in peace or receive some kind of succour, some comfort from being here, that this place should be like that.'

Despite the often dismal reputation that shelters have for being sites of victimization, shelter workers strive to create refuges for clients. In the words of a shelter manager in Vancouver, 'what we can do is try to make this place a sanctuary, make this place a kind of stronghold.' Similarly, a worker in a shelter in Montreal states that 'a lot of women feel safe here. Why? Because they know their problems out there won't get involved in here … and actually they are more safer in here.'

In their attempts at creating safe havens for clients, service organizations have begun to utilize a variety of physical-security measures. Chief among these are forms of access control that limit entry to a facility or circumscribe the ability to move freely through the premises. Intercoms, closed-circuit television (CCTV) cameras, card-key entry, and door staff are all variously employed, singly or in combination, in order to control access. At one shelter in Edinburgh, my colleague and I found ourselves pressing an intercom to speak to a receptionist under the gaze of a CCTV camera. Once we had identified ourselves and explained why we were there, we were buzzed into the lobby area and greeted by a receptionist sitting next to a bank of CCTV monitors. We were then required to sign a visitor's registration form that asked our names, the day and time, whom we were there to see, and the purpose of our visit, before being directed to sit and wait for the manager to come and fetch us. Access-control policies at this particular shelter were so stringent that, according to one shelter client, 'you are only allowed to go out once to go have a cigarette.' The use of registers to record visitor activities is common. A shelter manager explains, 'It means that I know everybody who's in the building and I know most of them by name, and I know who's likely to cause a problem … it's to stop these predators from coming in, because there are people who will prey on the weak and the hungry' (Huey 2008: 216).

CCTV surveillance systems have become ubiquitous within community facilities. When asked the purpose of the cameras, service providers offer various security-related reasons centred on tracking the movement of individuals, investigating incidents, and for general deterrence. For instance, a service provider in Vancouver explains the use of CCTV within her facility as follows: 'For us it's mainly tracking movement, because upstairs there's nobody supposed to be out' and 'there's safety issues around keeping others out of the facility that shouldn't be in there.' In relation to thefts within the shelter, she also views the security tapes as useful because 'anything happens, it's there.' Similarly, a representative of another service agency in Vancouver's DTES asserts that

Photograph 5.1 Gated shelter yard (Toronto)

cameras within her facility assist staff in investigating reported thefts, harassment, and other incidents: 'We've had clients say there was this guy, girl, who was talking to me and this is what happened. Maybe nobody really saw it, maybe they don't even know who the person was, but then we can go through and go, "Okay, let's check on the cameras."' Even facilities that have no internal cameras often have at least one external camera trained on their entrance.

Clients are aware of the CCTV cameras in facilities and often see them as a beneficial security tool (Huey 2010). A female residing in a mixed-use shelter is one of those individuals who is happy about the presence of cameras within local shelters: 'There's the front desk. All the viewing screens are there. I can go right now and show you every floor, everyone. I know that they are being monitored, because I can see that they're being monitored.' Another resident of this same shelter says, 'We all know that there is a security guy and we see the screens and we see the cameras and we see that it is being watched.' When residents of shelters in Vancouver and Toronto are asked whether the presence of cameras

Photograph 5.2 Shelter CCTV sign and camera (Toronto)

within service facilities makes them feel safer, the majority reply in the affirmative: cameras 'make people think' before committing an offence, one woman notes, while yet another interviewee says of the shelter she is residing in, 'You can guarantee that if there were no cameras here, I wouldn't be here' (ibid.: 72).

Policies, rules, and guidelines determine not only who will be admitted to a facility but shape behaviour within it (Huey 2008; Johnsen et al. 2005). 'What happens inside the building is our beef,' a shelter manager in Vancouver explains. 'If you come in here you need to abide by the rules.' Clients are generally abjured to abstain from illegal activities while on the premises, as well as from any behaviour that might be deemed inappropriate or offensive to staff or other patrons. Prohibited behaviour generally includes substance use, dealing drugs, aggressive or threatening language or conduct, and acts of violence. In order to ensure conformity to site rules, service facilities adopt strategies for identifying and responding to problems, as well as enforcing rules through a range of sanctions. For potential problems or minor issues, simply speaking to the person and asking them to modify the behaviour is frequently a first response. Some facilities have what they call a 'chill out' room in which volunteers and staff can calm clients down in order to prevent situations from escalating. Other responses to broken rules include confiscation of dangerous or banned items, verbal warnings, or asking a client to leave for the day. Repetitive problems or rule infractions deemed sufficiently serious by staff are also frequently dealt with through the imposition of a ban from service. Bans can be permanent or for a specified period of time; they are justified by service organizations on the ground that such actions serve to protect clients from predation. 'Yes, we see it, where one person in the shelter victimizes another ... well, when he comes back the next time he wants to stay in the shelter, "Sorry, you ripped somebody off and I'm not letting you back in to rip off more people,"' explains a shelter worker in Vancouver. 'The problem is he'll do it to three and four more people, and I can't have him putting a whole bunch of people through misery.' In order for bans to be effective, they have to be actively enforced by service staff, which is often tricky when dealing with a banned individual who is insistent on acquiring access or resources. This point is made clear in the following story from a service provider in Edinburgh:

> A very well-known, notorious service user ... he came in on Sunday night and I'm always kind of wary and watching him. He started to get a bit ... shouting and swearing and that, so one of my volunteers ... went over and said to him, 'Right. Calm down. Stop acting like that.' So he didn't and Joe[3] said to him, 'I want you to leave.' So at that point I became aware that there was something going on and Joe was asking him to go. He got very aggressive towards Joe, I think really to show me how tough he was ... so I barred him. He was barred for a month, and away he went. Came back the following night. I said, 'You can't come in.' He said, 'I've just come back to apologize.' I said, 'That's great, very big of you. I'm genuinely very grateful that you came back to apologize. That's the right thing to do.' 'So, am I getting in?' 'No' [laughs]. He didn't like that, he said, 'But I've apologized.' 'And I accept your apology, but there's still a consequence. You need time to reflect on your behaviour and modify it. And when that happens, you can come back in. You've been barred for a month.' 'But I'm really hungry.' I said, 'Sorry, but that's not my fault.' He said, 'Go and get me a meal.' 'No.' 'Go on, I'll just eat it here. At the front door.' 'No.' Eventually, because I'm really soft, I said, 'I'll go and get you a sandwich.'

So I go and got him a sandwich and while I was out in the kitchen, he tried to get in!

In their quest to make their shelter a safe haven for clients, workers in Vancouver created an internal reporting system that allows people to fill out incident reports. Since the shelter has, in the words of its manager, 'cameras everywhere,' 'if anything bad happens it can be documented ... and that person can be barred from the facility for life, if they're bad enough. Otherwise, it would be you're not allowed to be back for a very long time.' However, since homeless citizens are heavily dependent on the services of community organizations, most will conform their behaviour rather than receive a banning (Huey 2007; Johnsen et al. 2005).

Community-Service Workers

I'm very quick to intervene in a situation which is developing, hopefully before it gets to the stage where there's an offence committed. The intervention takes place and the offence doesn't happen.

– Service provider, Edinburgh

Within service facilities, policies and technological devices are only part of the security equation related to service provision. An equally important component is the human factor: the informal security-related functions that community-service workers take on in order to meet the needs of their clients (Huey 2009). They often become trusted figures within the community and, as such, clients will turn to them in situations where they feel threatened or have been victimized, seeking assistance or a solution to their problem. Assistance seeking is exemplified in the words of a homeless volunteer at a service facility in Edinburgh who states: 'Depending on who you trust, who you speak to. I mean I've been in trouble, and if I've needed a wee bit of help I've sat there and explained the situation to [names a service provider], and he'll go away and see such and such. And then he'll come back to us. "Do you have any answers for us?" He's got answers' (cited in Huey 2008: 214–15). When asked whom she would report victimization to, if anyone, a female shelter resident in Vancouver advises that 'there's a couple staff members here that I feel more than comfortable going and telling them anything' (Huey and Quirouette 2009: 41). Other homeless citizens express similar views:

A: I just don't talk to the police. That's it. I just don't talk to cops at all. That's the bottom line.

Q: What about the staff? Do you have a better relationship with them?

A: Oh yeah. The staff at all the drop-ins and all the shelters are A-1, man.

Q: You trust them?

A: Oh, definitely.

A Vancouver woman says that, because of her trust in the shelter workers in the facility she resides in, she feels a greater level of comfort in the idea of revealing victimization to them than to police: 'As far as comfort zone goes, I would talk to any one of these workers here before I ever go down to the police station.'

Service providers acknowledge that they often receive reports of victimization, as well as information from clients concerning dangers within the community. 'That happens a lot,' a service worker in Vancouver states of such reports (ibid.). Another shelter worker says, 'It's not uncommon for clients to come to us if they're scared' (ibid.). In some situations, clients are unsure what has happened to them or what potential avenues for assistance are available to them, so they turn to a trusted service worker for guidance. In the following story, a community-service worker in Edinburgh tells of a young woman who sought advice on how to deal with an incident of victimization where she was unsure as to what had happened:

> A girl came to me on Saturday night and told me that she had been out last Tuesday night, on her own, drinking. Doesn't remember anything that happened. Woke up three days later, on a Friday, in a flat, away on the south side of the City. Boarded up, empty flat. And she has no recollection what happened to her for those three days. Doesn't know who she was with. Doesn't know how she got there. She had money taken from her and her phone taken. But that's all she had. Doesn't know if she was raped ... one of the suggestions that I had was go to the police. But for her, in that situation, it was about how does she begin to put her life back together? I think she felt really powerless to do anything about it, because she didn't know, she didn't remember anything.

A significant component of clients' trust in community-service workers is the extent to which service providers are known for exercising discretion and maintaining confidences. To maintain trust, service workers have to be judicious with respect to decisions about when to report incidents to the police. For the most part, except for situations involving immediate violence or serious violent offences, service providers tend to deal with situations informally – that is, without police involvement. They talk to both parties in a dispute, issue warnings, maintain informal surveillance of a person, place, or situation, and threaten sanctions. It is the track record of individual service workers in maintaining confidences and dealing with situations informally that is one of the primary reasons many homeless victims of crime prefer to report incidents to them rather than to police or other authorities (Huey 2007; Huey and Quirouette 2009). In the words of a man interviewed in Edinburgh, homeless citizens who are fearful over potential or actual criminal threats 'are more apt to come and talk about things like that' with service workers. He explains that, by doing so, they hope to 'alleviate some of the problems that they might have, without involving the police like that.'

Although service workers are often loath to call the police, in some situations – where individuals represent a danger to themselves or to others – they may have little choice. One such incident is described by a service worker in San Francisco: 'We had a situation here on Tuesday where someone was taken into custody ... he picked up a chair ... We called the police to get help ... He went off on the police as well. I mean, first they didn't believe me and they weren't going to put him in custody because he hadn't hurt anybody. But I told them, you know, when you pick up a chair and you raise it over your shoulder ...' In this particular instance, the decision to call the police was made on the basis of the service worker's concern that the individual with the chair might himself be attacked by others, escalating the violence. As he explains, 'we had people that pulled the chair down but I made a citizen's arrest for two reasons. One was so that he wouldn't hurt anyone else, but the other was so that he wouldn't get beaten up. He was ready to be pounced on by a whole bunch of people because he had threatened people and he was verbally antagonistic.' Service workers' ability to exercise discretion can also be limited by policies mandating police involvement in certain situations. For example, a manager of one shelter in Edinburgh notes that, because of policy, 'if we become aware of any incident that has happened, like we have in the past [when] a fight broke out, we call the police.'

While some service organizations specifically employ staff to provide security services on-site, many service workers function in multiple roles that include informal policing tasks. One of these tasks is site surveillance. Shelter operators and other facility managers are keenly aware of the fact that victimization takes place within their own and other service organizations. Thus, staff members are expected to monitor and record the behaviour of service users and look for unusual or suspicious individuals and activities in order to prevent theft, drug dealing, harassment, and assault on-site. To identify someone who might be dealing drugs on the premises, staff might look for any individual 'who was not popular previously and has suddenly become popular' (Huey 2008: 216). To prevent prohibited behaviour, some service workers check rooms, follow suspect individuals, and observe client interactions. According to a male shelter client in Toronto, in at least one facility, service workers even monitor bathroom stalls: 'Well, here's the problem: in these kinds of places, we're not the "crème de la crème" of society. People use drugs. It becomes an issue of not watching for crime, but watching who is doing drugs ... I sat here last night. Two in the morning. There is a staff member at the washroom door, watching underneath the stalls, to see what people are doing.' Although such intrusive monitoring can have practical security benefits, this individual concludes that observing behaviour in bathrooms in this instance is 'not for your protection, it's for the staff to find you doing something bad.'

In discussing the nature of their security-related work, a recurring theme in interviews with service providers is peacekeeping. When disputes between clients occur, service workers engage in dispute-resolution tactics in order to avert potential violence. A soup-kitchen manager in Edinburgh says that one of his tactics is to confront people directly about harassing or bullying behaviour: 'There are a small number of people who will come in and will try to be [shrugs] ... and it's quite pathetic, they'll try to be top dog in a soup kitchen. And I'll pull them aside and say, "Look, what are you doing? What are you trying to do? Be a top man in a soup kitchen? Get a hold of yourself. That's not a very brave, smart thing to be. That doesn't really make you a tough guy. You're not a gangster if the most you can do is bully people at a soup kitchen."'

With robbery one of the most common forms of victimization experienced by homeless citizens, staff at some service facilities escort clients off-site in order to ensure their safety. For example, a service provider in Vancouver states that, 'on welfare day, I'll take somebody who's in the shelter – if they want to walk to the welfare office – I'll walk them to the welfare office and to the bank and then I'll walk them back here.' In Edinburgh, a shelter worker advises that, with elderly or frail clients, 'we'll go with them to pick up their money.' In Toronto, a community-service worker says that, to prevent being robbed or rolled, her clients, 'when they get a cheque, some will even come to me and give it to me to hold. Some of them come when they are intoxicated, and leave the money.'

Security?

We help each other.

– Homeless male, Edinburgh

It's like one woman steals another woman's cell-phone and clothing, and then she gets her friends to beat her up, and all you get is this cycle of violence and all that anybody ever got out of it was a five dollar rock.

– Service provider, Vancouver

As with other modes by which homeless citizens seek security, relying on others for security is not a proposition without some significant limitations. For example, while friendship is treated as a currency on the street, the harsh reality is that people tend to be most victimized by those they trust (Gaetz 2004; Huey and Quirouette 2009). Thus, there is the experience of the elderly man who was 'set up' for a robbery by a friend who knew where his money was stashed, and the experience of the man who was 'piped down' in another robbery by a friend he had known for some five years. So normal are such betrayals within many street-based communities that, when I once asked a man who had been rolled by a friend why he continued the relationship, he responded that he saw such predatory behaviour as simply a cost of friendship.

This cost is also one that is frequently borne by those who seek protection through intimate partnerships. As homeless women acknowledge, many of the partners who are turned to for protection and intimacy are 'not very good for them' (Huey and Berndt 2008: 187). Fear drives some women who are new to the streets to seek out a partner regardless of whether he is, in the words of one woman, 'a good guy, a bad guy, whatever' (ibid.: 187). A frequent result is that women seeking security through such relationships are often exploited, as well as physically and sexually abused, by those they trust the most (Tyler and Johnson 2004).

Examining the question of how to address potential dangers associated with high-risk activities on the streets reveals the limits of the current institutional, legal, and cultural frameworks currently in place. In an effort to fill the security gap that exists with respect to work in the sex trade, citizens involved in this economic activity attempt to employ various harm-reduction strategies, such as engaging in the practice of 'spotting.' Unfortunately, though, because of the nature of the act and the legal environment surrounding it, it is likely that at some point the sex worker will be in an unobservable space, with few means of protection or opportunities for escape (Shannon et al. 2008). At best, the information produced through spotting can be used retroactively to investigate an attack (if reported) or to create a 'bad date' sheet to be circulated through the community.

Community spaces often serve as refuges for those seeking to get away from the chaos, disorder, and violence that frequently characterize the streets. In relation to those sites that are specifically set up to provide services for homeless populations, administrators create rules and policies, as well as utilizing staff and physical-security devices, as ways of facilitating order and reducing crime within. Yet victimization still occurs within these sites and security measures and devices often do little to deter thievery, assault, and other crimes. Ultimately, the most effective tool that site administrators have is the ban, but it is not unreasonable to suggest that banning patrons does little more than displace crime from one space to another.

In this chapter I also considered the extent to which service providers act informally as community police, taking reports of victimization, counselling victims, resolving disputes, and, in some instances, physically guarding vulnerable clients. In 2008, when Marianne Quirouette and I launched the study of remote reporting,[4] all service providers and homeless citizens interviewed were asked about the extent to which there were trust relations between the two groups. In other words, do homeless service users trust service providers and would they be willing to confide in them about potential dangers and/or incidents of victimization? For the most part, both groups replied affirmatively (Huey and Quirouette 2009). However, this was not always the case and some service users stated unequivocally that they did not trust staff at the facility they were accessing. We are not alone in this finding: S. Gaetz (2004) similarly notes that few street youth in his study in Winnipeg report criminal victimization to community-service providers and other 'authority figures.'

One potential solution for increasing security within homeless communities might be to take a page from those who promote community responsibilization strategies and attempt to organize local communities to respond collectively to safety and security threats. Such efforts are not unheard of. In the early 2000s, residents of San Francisco's Tenderloin community organized a restorative justice program aimed at addressing issues related to low-level offending, mostly involving 'quality of life.' Not only did area residents assist in running the program, but they also sat as judge-arbiters who had a direct say in how issues are dealt with in their community. In Vancouver a local 'safety office' was run for many years out of the DTES by a staff of local volunteers. However, while such initiatives have had some success, generally there are three issues that work against their long-term viability.

First, both of the programs noted above were complements to the existing criminal justice system and were organized with the support and resources of local police and other state authorities. As we know, those homeless citizens who adhere to the 'code of the street' or have other reasons to be sceptical of, or antagonistic towards, state authorities are not likely to participate in such efforts, preferring instead to 'just deal with it.' Thus, the reach of programs of this kind can be rather limited. Second, despite the presence of some heartening success stories, most homeless communities still lack the capacity to take on the burden of such projects (Huey and Quirouette 2009; Herbert 2007). For residents, there is often a daily struggle just to find food or shelter or to deal with mental-health or addiction-related issues. With respect to the community projects referenced above, two of the primary organizers were in low-income housing in their respective communities and thus had some measure of daily stability in their lives. However, this is clearly not the case for many other potential volunteers. Without the active and ongoing participation of invested local participants, as well as guaranteed sources of funding from outside the community, such projects often just wither away over time (Huey 2007) – as happened to the two examples cited.[5] Looking to community-service providers to provide financial, resource, and other support for security-oriented local programs is also not a viable option. Many such organizations are already hard-pressed to manage their existing caseloads, services, and facilities without the additional burden of new programs (Huey and Quirouette 2009).

In short, it bears repeating: options for acquiring security are highly circumscribed when one is homeless. Homeless citizens are forced to seek out avenues for accessing security through the limited means available to them, and attempting to find security through others is one such strategy. As it happens, on the streets the promise of finding security through others turns out to be largely illusory.

6 Security and the Homeless Citizen

It's sort of written into our society at the moment that, to a certain degree, you don't take 'those people' [the homeless] seriously … you hide behind this saying that 'they don't take responsibility or contribute to society necessarily,' and that's the reason you're allowed to ignore them.

– Homeless female, Toronto

I once got lost in San Francisco. After spending some spent time walking in circles, I came across a small squat building that had all the hallmarks of a police station. So I went in and asked for help. This was in 2000.

Fast forward three years and I have a meeting one morning at the San Francisco Police Department's community police station in the Tenderloin district. I go to the door, push it, and remain firmly on the outside. Looking about, I spot a camera overhead and an intercom. I buzz it, explain my business, and am granted entry into a stark, concrete waiting room, where I sign a register provided by a police officer who is safely tucked away behind bullet-proof glass.

I didn't give either experience much thought until I subsequently interviewed two homeless men I had met at a local drop-in centre. Over coffee, the men answered my questions and told stories about living in the Tenderloin. One thing both were both particularly adamant about was that it was pointless ever to go to the police for any reason. To illustrate why, they tell of an incident that occurred to one of them over unpaid drug debts, when a dealer sent some 'enforcers' to secure payment. When their target saw the enforcers coming, he took off running:

A1: Hey look, I ran to the cops. I ran to the precinct when it was at that bank, that bank they turned into a precinct. I had like six guys chasing me.

I jumped in the back of a pickup truck at a stoplight and said, 'Drive man! Drive!' He looked back, he saw them guys coming, he took me down to the police centre. I jumped out, and I had to ring a bell! I had to ring a bell and nobody answered!

A2: On camera and everything.

A1: And they beat the crap out of me in front of the police station.

A2: Nah, it was around the corner.

A1: I figured they weren't going to answer the door. I mean, they answered the door when they locked me up the last time!

The irony of the situation is fairly striking: presumably the San Francisco police opened a community police station in the Tenderloin to reduce crime in the neighbourhood and keep residents safe. And yet police feel the need to limit residents' access to the building in order to increase the security of officers inside. So while the police, with their self-defence training, guns, batons, and CCTV cameras, sit behind bullet-proof glass, residents are denied free access to *their* community police station and to the occupants who are supposed to serve and protect *them*. This story, perhaps more than any other I could draw upon, speaks to the unequal nature of security provision within contemporary societies. In the instant that the doors of his community police station remained closed to him, this man's status as a 'lesser citizen' was confirmed.

How Do Homeless Citizens View Security?

There's a lot of homeless, they don't feel safe walking the streets at night.
– Homeless male, Toronto

On perusing the literature on homelessness and criminal victimization, an intriguing paradox appears: several researchers have cited findings suggesting that, despite higher rates of victimization among the homeless individuals surveyed, their study participants sometimes express lower levels of concern for their security. For example, in a study of homeless individuals who are mentally ill – a highly vulnerable group – researchers found that 'unexpectedly, the level of perceived vulnerability to victimization was lower than actual victimization' (Hiday et al. 1999: 65). V. Hiday and his colleagues further noted that, in answering questions about individual safety, almost 60 per cent stated that they were satisfied with their level of physical security, whereas only about 16 per cent stated they felt at risk of victimization (ibid.: 65). Similarly,

M. Kipke et al. (1997: 366) found that, among homeless youth surveyed, 'the rates of fear of victimization were not as high as one might expect.' Despite the fact that homeless youth typically experience high rates of violent victimization, 60 per cent of respondents in the Kipke study reported that they were 'not at all afraid' of being physically assaulted and 54 per cent expressed similar views over the possibility of being sexually assaulted. From such results, one could reasonably conclude that security and its acquisition is not a significant issue for homeless citizens. I want to tackle this paradox before turning to the larger question of whether security actually matters to those among us who are homeless.

In an article on the politics of fear, social theorist Tom Pyszczynski (2004: 827) offers the following observation: 'Fear and anxiety are two of the most intolerable emotions we humans are capable of experiencing.' So how, then, do we understand the paradox of high rates of victimization in homeless communities coupled with lower reported rates of fear? Pyszczynski (2004) offers a viable answer when he notes of the human relationship with fear that 'people will do almost anything to avoid being afraid. When despite their best efforts these feelings do break through, people go to incredible lengths to shut them down' (ibid.: 827). One means by which individuals can tamp down feelings of fear and anxiety is by actively taking steps to reduce their risk of victimization, thus creating the potential not only for increased physical security but for ontological security as well (Coston 2004). To that end, as described in the previous chapters, we find many homeless citizens adopting security measures. The fact that they do so can only be interpreted as indicating that security does indeed matter for this group of individuals.

Another means of reducing one's fears is using processes of rationalization to diminish or deny perceived threats (Kipke et al. 1997; Coston 2004). For instance, a young man interviewed in Toronto says, 'I can't see myself being victimized.' When asked if he has observed a lot of crime and violence on the streets of Toronto, another homeless male replies, 'No, no, most of the time it's pretty relaxed, it's pretty solid … it's pretty serene down here; it's well controlled.' This fellow later contradicts his own characterization of life on the streets several times, particularly when he notes his own experiences of victimization, which included having been randomly attacked with a two-by-four plank and being robbed at knifepoint. When asked for his observations about victimization of those who are homeless, another male in Toronto responds dismissively: 'I see a couple of arguments, that's about it.' However, when he is subsequently asked about whether Toronto should install more public CCTV surveillance cameras in the downtown core, where his shelter is located, he excitedly replies, 'They should have cameras on our street. It's the worst street!' (Huey 2010: 74). In case his message has somehow been lost on the interviewer, he adds, 'It's bad, I'm telling you!'

In discussing the common refrain of 'you deal with it,' heard with depressing regularity from so many homeless victims of crime, Julia Wardhaugh (2000: 93) suggests that this expression reveals 'complex psychological processes at work, wherein assumption of victim status or identity is not tenable when vulnerability to further victimisation is continued, and when the need to emphasise strength and survival is urgent.' Such processes can be seen in the words of a homeless male in Toronto who suggests that access to police services may be necessary 'for some people.' He is quick to add that such services are needed by others, 'not for me.' Similarly, other males and a few females advise, in the words of one fellow from Edinburgh, that all victims need to do to resolve their situation is 'man up.' Displaying bravado is, as discussed previously, a time-honoured security strategy on the streets. That people would enact tough guises, even in a research setting, is not surprising given that such postures represent not only a defensive strategy but also a psychological shield for surviving in an often harsh environment. A man in Vancouver acknowledges the use of this shield, framing it as a gendered defence: 'We think we can deal with it ourselves and most of us do. We do. That's just the male ego.' Dropping this guise to reveal weakness or vulnerability, as well as consciously examining the fact that one remains within a precarious environment, would likely not only invoke those feelings one seeks to diminish but also create an intolerable state of cognitive dissonance within individuals (Kipke et al. 1997).

Still other homeless citizens 'deal with' victimization and its threat by becoming apathetic, a condition that has been described by at least one homelessness researcher as the result of a 'realistic assessment of their situation – a hopeless and unpredictable situation' (Vance 1995: 65).[1] When asked how he would respond to victimization, a male in Toronto says that he would 'just leave it.' His explanation for this response is to say, 'My lifestyle … it's just different.' Another male in Toronto replies, 'I would just forget it.' Still another individual explains victimization as 'part of life.' Service providers who work with homeless populations also note apathetic responses to the threat of victimization, responses borne of previous experiences of being invisible victims. For instance, a service provider who works with women in Vancouver's sex trade explains of her clients: 'A lot of the times the people that are being victimized, they feel they have to accept this.' Another service worker states: 'In the case of the sex trade worker, they'll think it happens because it's their job.' A shelter worker in Vancouver says that 'a lot of the women get abused nightly, in some form or shape. And they just accept it, because this is what they do and this is what happens. Would we? No. We have a job and home. They have nothing.' A shelter worker in Toronto describes her clients as feeling 'all the time vulnerable and at risk,' which she suggests develops into 'an unhealthy norm that is accepted.' When we asked a service provider in Edinburgh whether homeless citizens there would report victimization to police or other authorities, she was quick to note how awareness of the deviant status homeless people carry, along with other barriers they face, has an inhibiting effect on speaking up when victimized: 'Some of the guys have so many barriers in their lives, and some of them are very obvious. I might look and smell weird and talk weird … there is frustration with being invisible. "The community doesn't care about me anyways, so who wants to hear about my problems?"' Such comments should not be interpreted to mean that individuals have no wish to be secure, but rather that apathy or resigned acceptance have become means of survival in situations in which people feel that they have no other alternatives (Ravenhill 2008).

In short, inferring anything about homeless citizens' attitudes about security using only fear-of-crime surveys or basic questions about perceptions of risk can be a less than useful exercise. Even interviewing service providers who work directly with homeless clients can sometimes produce misleading results. For example, when shelter and other social-service workers were asked in 2008 about security as a basic need of their clients, several were adamant that basic subsistence – access to food, water, and shelter – were such overwhelming issues in the lives of their clients that security would fall far down the list of clients' needs. This view is entirely understandable, particularly given that hunger, lack of shelter, and addiction can be significant factors in driving desperate people to forsake basic precautions and place themselves in risky situations. However, when homeless citizens are asked directly about security-related issues, the answer as to where security fits in relation to the homeless citizen's hierarchy of needs is quickly discovered to be highly contingent on the individual and their specific situation.

Certainly, for some homeless citizens, security may be less of an issue because other needs clearly outweigh safety considerations. Yet many others see security as a basic need, which, if satisfied, will lead to having other needs and wants met. When in 2008 Marianne Quirouette and I asked homeless men and women if security – in particular the ability to access policing services to prevent victimization or respond to it – was important, 'yup' was the most frequent response. We also received a number of interesting comments. For example, a woman in Vancouver says that security is important 'so you can feel safe,' adding, 'There's a lot of homeless, they don't feel safe walking the streets at night after a certain time, let's say.' When asked why that feeling of security is important for an individual citizen, she explains that it is necessary 'for a person's general well-being … so they don't have these butterflies.' 'So, reducing the fear?' 'Yeah.' A man in Toronto opines that security 'might be important' for some homeless citizens in order 'to feel like they have some control.' A man in Vancouver believes that it is important for people to be able to 'have a safe and kosher day by knowing that you can go to bed tonight and not worry' about being criminally victimized. When asked to clarify if he means that everybody has a right to be safe, he responds, 'Exactly! People that have their houses or homes too. Everybody.' One particularly thought-provoking answer is provided by a woman in Vancouver who sees security as fundamental to a person's ability to alter their life conditions:

> I think any person, any human being, no matter where you are in life, has to feel safe in order to make good decisions for the rest of your life. Cuz one: as long as you're in a position of feeling like you've got to defend yourself you can never move forward. You can never get out of this, this circle of homelessness. You can only get out of it if you feel safe. So, once you get yourself into a position of safety for a certain length of time, you can start making better decisions towards a better life. If you're always in that I have to defend myself and I have to keep my guard up and I can trust no one, you'll never ever move forward. Ever. It's a primal instinct to protect yourself.

When asked about the need for physical security – for example, being able to call the police or to walk safely down a street – she links physical security to ontological security, suggesting that both can lead to self-actualization: 'Somebody who feels safe is going to, I mean … I think people who do amazing things in the world, you know, Mother Theresa, always felt safe within herself and do you know what? She probably worked in some pretty terrible conditions.' This individual was not the only respondent to see security in terms of possibilities related to self-actualization. A man in Toronto advises that he was seeking admittance to a particular shelter because it was a safe environment and therefore a space in which he could work to get himself 'into a better position [in life].'

Conversely, living in a constant state of insecurity takes a significant physical and psychic toll on the individual. 'When your own being is threatened, I think it's primal instinct to protect it and it's debilitating,' a woman in Vancouver explains. 'You cannot do anything else, ever! Make no decision, not even maybe what to wear that day, until that need is met!' Providing a sense of security is seen as especially important for those individuals who have already been traumatized by violent victimization, as one man in Vancouver notes: 'I think there should be a support system for every kind of abuse or assault or anything, because it's all different. Especially with sexual assault, people need that security or that reinsurance that it wasn't their fault and that everything's going to be okay.' What both of these respondents were referring to are the physical, mental, and emotional costs of living in insecurity.

The Costs of Insecurity

[To not] feel safe in your own home, that's a horrible feeling regardless of where your home is.

– Service provider, Vancouver

When academics discuss the victimization of marginalized groups, we often do so within the context of crime rates or, as in the analysis in this book, within a framework that sees victimization as simply another manifestation of a degraded social status. In the paragraphs that follow, I want to shift the discussion slightly by exploring the financial, physical, and mental costs associated with living in a state of insecurity. Some of those costs are the direct result of victimization, others are the result of living with the fears that the violence of street life frequently engenders.

As we saw earlier, when I once asked a man in San Francisco if anyone would ever report a crime to the police, his immediate response was to laugh bitterly. 'Why? It's not like they're going to scour the town because one junkie ripped another junkie off" (Huey and Kemple 2007: 2311). In this brief sentence he aptly characterized a predominant view of the victimization of the homeless citizen, one in which the victim is rendered invisible because he or she is seen as having no social value, and thus victimization entails no financial, physical, mental, or emotional costs. In this view, his or her status as homeless negates the need for any action on the part of the police or other authorities. In a similar

vein, people are sometimes surprised to find that theft is the most common form of victimization reported by those who are homeless, and that
pilfering is rampant in shelters and other service facilities. Such losses
are frequently dismissed because of the perception that homeless individuals have little or nothing of value to steal and their losses are therefore insignificant. The rejoinder to such a view is amply offered by a
homeless man who explains how economies of scale work: 'If someone
steals your ten dollars, that's your life. You might not have a place to
sleep tonight.' For one young homeless woman in Montreal, while the
theft of her bag had few financial consequences, her attachment to it
meant that its loss was experienced on an emotional level: 'I didn't have
anything in it. But you know it's my home, my bag. I need my fucking
bag.' A police officer explains, 'They are getting their stuff stolen … stuff
that you and I would look and go "uhhhhhh, that is not important," but
that is their worldly possessions.' Similarly, an officer in Toronto advises
that 'a lot of people take their stuff with them in little shopping carts
and, to them, that's everything they've got in the whole wide world and
it's very precious to them. Sometimes there may be stuff in there that's
valuable. It may not be valuable for us but it's valuable to them. For
example, maybe twenty tin cans, but they can only get five cents for
them so it's worth a dollar. Somebody else could come along and say
"I'll take them," assault that person, and take those tin cans. It's not a
lot for ourselves, but for somebody who's about day after day trying to
get their stuff together, a dollar's a lot.'

Physical and sexual violence also produce both physical and mental
costs for victims that are too easily dismissed by those outside homeless
communities. Sometimes homeless victims are rendered invisible because people's disgust over the physical or social state of a homeless
victim engenders disbelief in onlookers that others would want to touch
them. They are, after all, constructed as both physically and socially
dangerous. A police officer makes this point in discussing the victimization of homeless women: 'I guess the public do not see victimization …
for the public to know that women are sexually assaulted and then they
say, "Who in God's name would want to do something like that?"' His
response? 'Take a look within yourself. There are a lot of them out there
that do that.'

While a physical assault might involve nothing more than shoving,
pushing, or a slap, many victims end up with serious injuries that
require medical or other treatment. In discussing homeless crime victims, a police officer in Toronto notes that 'we see a lot of them out there

that are badly battered. "Oh, what happened?" "Oh, I got punched out or I got attacked at the shelter."' A woman in Toronto was injured when a jealous acquaintance decided to put a shard of broken glass into a crack pipe which went through her finger, requiring both stitches and follow-up treatment when the wound became infected. Another young man in Edinburgh was attacked by a group of young drunks and 'lost my teeth.' When we met him at a shelter in the Cowgate, he was in need of extensive dental work to repair the damage to the front of his mouth. And consider again some of the cases mentioned in previous chapters. The older man in Toronto who was beaten during a robbery describes his attack: 'I was grabbed from behind, put in a choke hold, knocked unconscious ... I was out cold.' This man, who says he is 'a sick man, bad back, bad heart,' states that upon regaining consciousness, 'all of a sudden [I] dropped, because my back is sore, my neck is still sore and my head was sore.' The young male in Toronto who was punched when he walked by someone in a shelter suffered a chipped tooth. The man who was 'piped down' in another robbery received two compound fractures in his arm. The man in Vancouver who was hit in the head with a piece of wood had to be hospitalized because the attacker 'smash[ed] my head ... cut my head open.' The woman in Vancouver who was the victim of repeated incidents of intimate partner violence describes her injuries as the result of having 'taken too many blows to the head from my first husband.' As a consequence of these assaults, 'I ended up getting a wheelchair.' The woman whose story is briefly told in the introduction to chapter 2 – she had been sexually assaulted and nearly murdered – ended up in the hospital and carries physical and emotional scarring as a result of her experiences.

In many instances, the effects of physical and sexual violence lead to mental and emotional problems for the victim. A woman who had been held captive by a former friend in order to force her boyfriend into securing drugs for the man was initially arrested because the police 'didn't know I was the victim,' before being freed. In describing the kidnapping and its aftermath, she references the mental and emotional injuries she sustained, noting, 'I was traumatized so much.' Another victim of intimate partner violence, who was mentioned in chapter 2, has been 'punched out four times in the eye' and 'got strangled' by an ex-fiancé whom she describes as her 'personal stalker.' As occurs with other victims of repeat violence, she is dealing with the emotional and mental strains engendered by constant threats and a system that seems incapable of dealing with the problem. 'I'm sick and tired of it,' she says.

'I'm to the point where I just want to give up and don't care.' However, some protective instinct remains, for she adds, 'But it's not safe for me to give up.'

Fear of further victimization is also a frequent result, which can have several negative consequences for the victim. In the DTES, residents speak of elderly citizens whose lives are circumscribed by the fact that they are often afraid to leave their hotel rooms or visit public spaces where they might be harassed, bullied, or assaulted. In Edinburgh, the situation is similar. In one area shelter a resident spoke of 'an us and them situation' in which 'the younger ones are kicking off [and] the older ones are afraid to come down for a cigarette where it's safe.' As this individual explains, elderly shelter residents 'would be down at 8 o'clock for their cup of tea or their coffee and they go outside for a cigarette before they go to their bed. Now they don't bother coming down, because they young ones have no money or they have got money, but they'll come up and say, "Do you have a cigarette?" So they find it's a form of intimidation, bullying. So they don't bother coming down anymore.' We interviewed one of those elderly residents, who was ecstatic about the fact that the following day he would be receiving permanent accommodation. Among the cited reasons for his happiness was the fact that he would no longer be subject to routine harassment.

On the streets, observing the victimization of others is an all too common occurrence for many homeless citizens (Buhrich et al. 2000). Witnessing violence can lead to the development of significant fears. For example, in responses to questions about crime and fear, a homeless woman in Montreal produces a list of individuals and scenarios – from young people wearing black clothes to drug addicts injecting in public – that she perceives as frightening based on what she has seen and learned on the streets. Of the people and situations that invoke her fears, she concludes, 'I am more afraid of the night, because there are gangs of people outside. You know there may be a gang of people and they may have already drank all that evening. And if you are out at midnight and they're standing on that corner, and there's four or five of them, it scares me.' This woman is afraid to leave the shelter and, as a consequence, her life is largely limited to what occurs within its walls. In describing the environment in which she lives, a woman in Toronto says, 'The violence, it can erupt at any time,' before giving a list of various incidents that she has either experienced or observed. Another woman in Vancouver notes that in a previous town she had 'seen brutal attacks on people.' When queried about these attacks, she tells a story of being stopped by police in a car with her sister and her sister's boyfriend and how the situation quickly escalated to the point where, when the sister tried to explain to the police that the boyfriend was becoming unglued because of an anxiety attack, the police 'grabbed her hair and started smashing her into where you get into the car,' leaving her face 'bloody.' Now, she says, she is afraid of police. For others, simply hearing stories of victimization over and over again produces fears, as in the case of a shelter worker in Montreal who has taken so many reports of victimization from her clients that 'when I go home at midnight, I am scared. I am afraid.'

For others, the experience of witnessing episodes of violence can lead to trauma. One woman in Vancouver witnessed a sex worker being abducted: 'Do you want to know how scared I felt? I was scared! I was really scared!' This individual says that she had been so afraid that she was unable to leave her SRO hotel room to find a phone and report the abduction until the following morning. She continues to live in fear that the offenders will return to her area or find out that she had reported them. Another woman relates the story of observing a security guard attack a man and knock him to the ground 'right in front of my feet.' The impact of this experience, she says, 'traumatized me and the man that it happened to ... the reason that I'm on mental disability is because of traumatization of things like this.'

As we know, many traumatized victims and witnesses do not report experiences to police or other authorities. As a result, they often do not receive appropriate medical or psychological counselling (Jasinski et al. 2005; Stermac and Paradis 2001). Failure to receive treatments post-victimization has repeatedly been demonstrated as having significant negative health and other consequences. Indeed, researchers have consistently noted links between symptoms of undiagnosed Post-Traumatic Stress Disorder and severe and/or multiple victimization among homeless citizens (North et al. 1994; Stewart et al. 2004; Whitbeck et al. 2007). For homeless women, experiences of violent and/or sexual assault greatly increase the likelihood that they will develop depressive symptoms, as well as substance-abuse problems (D'Ercole and Struening 1996; Padgett and Streuning 1992; Tucker et al. 2005). One woman interviewed in Montreal exemplifies the latter group. To deal with her fears over the possibility of being victimized while living in a women's shelter, she has turned to prescription medication, which she acknowledges is a problematic means of coping:

When I first got here I was really, really scared. Cuz you start hearing things about, okay they were in prison and they tried to do this and that and I am like, 'Oh my.' So it really scared the shit out of me. And now I am, like, used to it, because I know so many of the people who are here, but still I do have my times when I do feel overly overwhelmed and sometimes I do, just to get away from all the problems, I do take something to calm me. I mean I don't drink, I don't do drugs, but I mean taking tranquilizers is a thing I do for me. For me it's a bad thing, it's not a good thing. But right now this is what I need right now. I feel like if I don't take anything I will go crazy.

In a study of homeless women's experiences of victimization and subsequent mental health, E. Ambrosio et al. (1992) found that almost two-thirds of the women in their sample reported having contemplated suicide in the year prior to the study; one-third stated that they had made a suicide attempt during the same period. Past experiences of violence have also been found not only to be a significant predictor of psychological distress for homeless women (Ingram et al. 1996) but also to worsen psychotic symptoms of those who are mentally ill (D'Ercole and Streuning 1990). These and other results cause researchers Julia Lam and Robert Rosenheck (1998: 683) to conclude that there is evidence to suggest that 'victimization perpetuates homelessness, lowers self-rated quality of life, and decreases the likelihood of employment.' These authors add, 'The data paint a picture in which clients with the most severe psychiatric symptoms, substance abuse problems, and criminal histories are caught in a vicious, reinforcing cycle of victimization and homelessness' (ibid.: 683). Other researchers similarly paint a grim picture of the effects of criminal victimization on the homeless citizen. Examining the experience of personal theft, S. Ballintyne (1999: 13) notes that 'repeated personal theft forces rough-sleepers further into daily survival and exclusion. It increases dependence on daily services. When it connects with other problems, such as mental health, drug or alcohol misuse, it makes the possibility of leaving the streets more remote.'

Homelessness and Citizenship

Q: Do you agree that, as citizens, everybody has the right to be protected?
A: We certainly do.

– Homeless man, Toronto

In examining the status of 'homeless' and 'citizen,' scholars have noted the often punitive treatment of those who are homeless by the larger society and accordingly have conceptualized this population as 'lesser citizens,' 'non-citizens,' or 'anti-citizens' (Rose 1999; Feldman 2004;

Arnold 2004). In this section, I want to move beyond what others say about the homeless citizen, considering instead how the homeless view themselves in relation to the concept of citizenship.

In 2008 homeless men and women were asked whether they see themselves as citizens and, as such, entitled to the full benefits of citizenship, including security. The majority of respondents said that their homeless status does not or ought not negate their standing as citizens. For example, in response to the question, 'Do you feel like a full citizen?' a homeless man in Toronto replies, 'Sure I do. Sure I am. I mean, we're all the same. The way the country is structured – it's a social country.' Another man in Toronto stated that he feels that he is a 'full citizen' '99 per cent of the time.' We were told that the other 1 per cent occurs when he receives negative treatment by police or the general public because of his socio-economic status.

I note that some homeless individuals frame their citizenship status using the dominant discourse of 'rights and responsibilities.' As an example, a man in Edinburgh says that he feels that he is a citizen and is entitled to public services, because prior to becoming homeless he was an employed person who 'had never been in trouble with the police other than driving offences.' In support of his view that he is a citizen, he also notes that 'I have paid my taxes since I left school.' A male shelter user in Toronto sees himself as a citizen because he is willing to report crimes to police. Similarly, in declaring herself a citizen, a woman from the same city is careful to note that she doesn't break the law. In her own words, she 'stays within the guidelines of being a good citizen.'

Conversely, some homeless citizens who have extensive criminal records for both petty and serious offences openly embrace criminal status, using it as a way to self-identify and orient their attitudes and behaviour. One such fellow in Edinburgh scoffed at the idea of reporting victimization: 'As a criminal, I don't just pick up the phone and phone the police' (Huey and Quirouette 2010: 288). Echoing views found within the larger mainstream culture, a recently paroled offender in the same city was of the view that individuals engaged in criminal lifestyles, such as himself, had forfeited the right to receive the benefits of citizenship, including state-based protections:

A: So again, according to my views, if he has been a criminal his whole life, he is simply paying the price. But if he is a straight peg he is entitled to call the police. If he is a straight peg, chances are 99 per cent of the time that he has worked most of his life paying taxes. So he has paid the police to protect him. Okay so maybe he is down on his luck and has not had a job

for a couple years, but he is still not a criminal. So he is entitled to pick up
the phone and call the police. That's my views as a criminal.

Q: So if you are a criminal you don't have the right to be protected by the
justice system?

A: Aye, aye, in my view, aye.

However, other self-identified 'criminals' feel differently about the question of whether they are citizens and are therefore entitled to be secure as a right of citizenship. Indeed, the following excerpt from an interview with another self-identified 'criminal' in Edinburgh demonstrates this opposing view:

Q: As a citizen the justice system is there to protect you right?

A: Yeah, I totally agree with that.

Q: Even if you are a criminal you have the right to be protected from other criminals?

A: Yeah, I agree with that.

Similarly, another recently paroled offender in Edinburgh states that 'we have rights as well; everybody's got their rights' in response to a query as to whether he should have the right to ask police for protection.

When you also ask homeless individuals if they feel entitled to the full benefits of citizenship, the responses are again generally in the affirmative. 'I have the right to be treated as equally as anyone else,' a male in Edinburgh states, 'being homeless or not.' Included among the positive rights homeless citizens believe they are equally entitled to is security – that is, the right to be safe within both public and private spaces. For instance, homeless men and women were asked whether they agreed with the position that 'regardless of being homeless, you have the right to be protected.' 'Yeah,' an interviewee in Toronto replies. 'All people have those rights,' another homeless male in Toronto states, adding that those rights necessarily include the right 'to be protected.' This right to security, as understood by homeless citizens, necessarily entails being able to access police services when threatened or victimized. When a male shelter resident in Edinburgh is asked if homeless people have the right to call police for help, his response is unequivocal: 'Yeah, they are; definitely, they are entitled to it.' When asked if she was entitled to this benefit of citizenship, a homeless woman in Vancouver responds, 'I do agree ... in every sense of the word.' A service provider in Toronto agrees with the position that security is not simply a civil liberty to be granted based on fulfilling citizenship responsibilities, but a basic human right: 'Everyone has to be secure in society. I think that the right to safety is a basic human right – safety and security, these are very basic human rights.'

The right to security is also seen by homeless citizens as including the right of victims to access the criminal justice system. To illustrate the security benefits that access to justice for victims could have for the individual and the community, one fellow in Toronto employs the example of 'some guys driving around picking up girls and beating the fuck out of them and raping them.' 'That guy should be known [so that he can be stopped],' he asserts, adding that while 'things like that never really go away,' 'every little bit helps' when it comes to making the streets safer. A woman in Vancouver states that victim access to policing services is important for the community 'because other people can get hurt.' Still others see the ability of victims to access the criminal justice system as not only a marker of citizenship but as something important to maintaining their sense of justice. 'You knew that the person who did it to you was in the wrong,' a man in Toronto explains, 'and it gives you some satisfaction that the law was on your side.' In discussing the need of homeless citizens to be able to access policing services when they have been victimized, a young homeless man in Toronto speaks to the role that such services can play in affirming the basic dignity of those whose voices often go unheard: 'Even if they don't give you back your ten dollars, at least someone is acknowledging you as a human being.'

Lesser Citizens

[Homeless] people who are victims are soon forgotten about. You know what I mean?

– Homeless male, Edinburgh

I have previously argued that security is a significant component of citizenship in liberal- democratic societies, the lack of which can only denote one's status as a 'lesser citizen' (Rose 1999). I now explore this argument further by examining what the security gap means to homeless men and women.

In asking homeless citizens about whether they feel entitled to security as a benefit of citizenship, most realize that what they are really being asked is to measure their idealized version of citizenship against their current lived reality. It also becomes obvious they are keenly aware of the security gap they face and the role that their homeless status plays in not only increasing their vulnerability to crime but also reducing their ability to address their risk of victimization. For instance, a homeless woman in Toronto references a recent event in which police did not attend a robbery call at a local store, drawing the inference that if police would not provide assistance to a business owner (a 'respectable citizen'), then she (a 'homeless person') could not expect their help: 'The other day a guy got robbed, and the police wouldn't even come. They thought the robber might have gone already. They wouldn't even come to the guy's store! Then who am I? I'm on the street with nothing!' For many citizens, including this woman, living without easily accessible forms of security creates a sense of helplessness and hopelessness. 'Who's gonna come and help me?' she asks. A service provider in Toronto illustrates the sense of helplessness that many of her clients feel when faced with their own inability to access security. In discussing a recent case involving a female crime victim, the worker notes that her client 'thinks that nobody can help her, that no system can help her.' Similarly, a shelter resident in Toronto decries the fact that, despite the role that the state is supposed to play in fostering citizens' physical security, 'the system does not protect people all the time. It does not … there's a lot of people hurting that get no protection or nothing. They suffer and [society lets] them suffer and that's wrong.'

To be clear: while homeless citizens are generally aware of the increased potential for victimization on the streets and the limited number of options available to them, not everyone perceives themselves as being equally vulnerable. Rather, as previously noted, some deny the potential for vulnerability by blunting their fears, and others pretend that they are invulnerable. In other words, though there is agreement as to the existence of a security gap, there are some differences in relation to how individuals view its potential for adverse effects for themselves and for others. However, regardless of where homeless individuals see themselves in terms of the security gap and their potential vulnerability, there is a common denominator in their views of what the gap means in relation to their own status as citizens. 'Basically, not even being treated like a person,' a young man in Edinburgh states. Another says, 'We don't exist. That's the best way I can describe it, we don't exist.' A homeless woman in Toronto echoes these sentiments in discussing how the other men and women she shares the streets with are treated: 'They are invisible. If something was to happen to one of them, [people] would just continue on their way. They are people, but people just rush by and think that they are "things." If that person was hurt, or injured, who is going to protect that person?' The police, whose responsibility it is to protect all citizens, are often seen as offering little assistance. Homeless citizens who do go to the police frequently complain that they often face difficulties in getting their complaints taken seriously. One such complainant is a man in Toronto who says that an officer was openly dismissive of his report of an assault by a security guard. He is left to conclude that, 'if you have a three-piece suit and an attaché case beside you, I'm sure [they would respond differently].' Clearly angry and offended, he adds, 'It shouldn't matter what the hell you look like or act like. The issue is the criminal act!' A beggar in Edinburgh similarly feels that he cannot turn to the police for help because he believes that his dual status as both homeless and a beggar makes the police see him as a criminal:

Q: And how does that make you feel?
A: It makes you feel more worthless than you already are.
Q: Well, the police are supposed to protect citizens' rights? So do you feel like you're not being treated like a citizen?
A: Yeah, basically not even being treated like a person.

In Toronto, as noted in chapter 3, another homeless male who has been victimized says of the police that when he approaches them, they are quick to suggest that he must be guilty of some wrongdoing. Their attitude 'makes you feel like you've done something wrong. Meanwhile, you've just got beat up or whatever. Seldom any sympathy. Not that you're looking for sympathy, but humanity.' And this is the crux of the matter: lack of security, particularly in light of the state's promise to provide security to each of its citizens, affirms in one of the most meaningful of ways that the homeless person is neither a citizen nor much of a human being in the eyes of the state or the larger society.

Summing Up the 'Gap'

The level of violence, the level of drugs on the streets, the open drug use on the streets and the cops just … whatever. They just don't care … a lot of it could be cleaned up. They just focus all the people here and if they need to get them, then they know where they'll be.

– Homeless man, San Francisco

Throughout the previous chapters of this book, I have attempted to provide readers with some sense of the extent to which the lives of homeless citizens are marked by chronic insecurity, much of it fuelled by the crime that plagues the streets. Simply put, the reality is that homeless individuals are more likely to be criminally victimized than other populations, with length of time on the streets increasing an individual's odds of being repeatedly victimized. Faced with the knowledge that the police often cannot or will not assist them, they adopt various individual and group strategies for reducing the potential for victimization. However, as I have also shown, there are significant limitations with many of the strategies employed, which is why victimization rates among those who are homeless remain high.

To help understand this problem, I have been employing the term 'security gap' to encompass two forms of interrelated lacunae. The first is that which exists when one compares the wide array of security options available to the general public to the very limited number of options available to the homeless citizen. The second aspect of this security gap is its subjective element – the affective distance between someone's lived reality and his or her ideal state of being. It is this second gap that I am most concerned with. As I have sought to reveal through the previous pages, homeless citizens correctly see their situation as another manifestation of their degraded socio-economic status. Moreover, many, if not most, homeless men and women see themselves as 'citizens.' They believe that, by virtue of this status, they are entitled to the full benefits of citizenship, including a right to live in a relative state of security regardless of the fact that they are also homeless. However, despite seeing themselves as citizens, members of this stigmatized group are aware that their desire to be seen and treated as full citizens remains an unattainable ideal. Indeed, this point was made explicitly by one frustrated homeless man in Toronto in response to questions about his sense of what he is entitled to as a citizen: 'You are talking in ideals.' This fellow does not need researchers asking him questions about how he feels about his place in the world in order to work out the fact that he inhabits, at best, the space of 'lesser citizen.' Indeed, he is reminded of this each time he is victimized and each time the police fail to take his reports seriously. I recall, too, the words of a homeless man in San Francisco previously cited. I'm paraphrasing here, but in essence his intent was to point out a disturbing truth: in the current economic and social climate, few people appear to care about 'one homeless bum ripping off another.' In other words, it is all too easy to dismiss the fear, pain, and suffering of homeless victims as simultaneously less than our own fears, pain, and sufferings and somehow a case of just desserts.

Security is a public good because it is necessary to the well functioning of individuals and collectives. However, it is a public good that has been subject to rationing and, through the creation of a private market, is now also treated as a positional good (Neocleous 2006). The result of these processes has not only been the widening of already existing gaps between the haves and have-nots – a matter often of little significance for the haves – but the entanglement of all in a zero-sum game that has the potential to ratchet up that which security is meant to tame: insecurity. This zero-sum game plays out by creating ever wider segments of society that live in fear because increasing numbers of spaces and people are constituted as unsafe. These spaces and people are deemed unsafe because they are. Why? One reason is that the citizens within those spaces lack the means or the capacity to generate security internally, as the previous chapters amply demonstrate. Another reason is that the state, which, because of its access to various forms of social, economic, political, and symbolic capital (Dupont 2004), is often the sole source capable of generating and anchoring security-building initiatives, often fails to do so. States fail in this task because their resources are highly rationed (Garland 1996), often along socio-economic lines (Ericson 2007).

The frequent result is that one group of citizens drives through 'the bad parts of town' with the doors of their Escalades carefully locked, while others are forced to live in those 'bad areas,' and often without doors to lock. The irony compounds when one considers that there would be significantly less need to remote-lock the car doors in *any* neighbourhood if greater numbers of citizens were willing to recognize the citizenship rights of those who are homeless and other disenfranchised groups, including a positive right to security. In essence, we would all benefit if we began to recognize that creating security necessarily entails providing security. Put another way, the treatment of security as a bona fide public good and the wider the distribution of this good will result in a greater number of those who can access forms of it, with more benefits to be accrued by all. I will have significantly more to say about redistributing security in the next chapter.

7 Equalizing Security

Our society has an obligation to protect [the homeless].
— Service provider, Toronto

When I landed back in Edinburgh in 2008, there was one person whom I was keen to reconnect with: the organizer of a local soup kitchen. I had met him during my previous fieldwork in 2003 and in 2008 he was still there, still doing the same work. When we first met, we had spent several hours talking about crime, victimization, policing, and the security of homeless citizens. In those days, and as he himself subsequently acknowledged, he had not considered the security of his clients – both within and outside his space – as a significant issue. Instead, his focus was on getting his service up and running, making sure there was food for his clients and volunteers to make things operate smoothly. Issues related to actual or potential victimization on the premises could be dealt with, he thought, on an ad hoc basis through informal internal peacekeeping practices. Five years later, much had changed.

When we sat down together in 2008, I began by asking him whether he still felt that it was never appropriate to call police to deal with victimization among clients. His response was as unflinchingly honest as I had come to expect: 'I think I've probably changed my attitude about that, I would say. I think it would depend on what the situation was. But if a person was being victimized, I think ... obviously in five years things have gone on ... five years ago I didn't know anything and I've probably learned a lot more in that time ... For us, now, probably the most important thing to me is that people who come in here feel safe within here.' Over the course of an hour, we discussed his shift in attitude towards client security and how this change was now reflected in his work. While talking about the various security-related policies he and his volunteers had enacted in order to 'make clients feel safer,' he started up his computer and began e-mailing me the documentation on these policies so that I could assess the changes for myself. Weeks later I sat down and started reading through these documents, paying particular attention to the rationales provided for policies implemented. In a document intended for distribution to clients,[1] I noted that visitors to the site were asked to refrain from anti-social behaviour in order to create a 'free and relaxed' space where people respect each other. I also observed that particular emphasis was placed on not engaging in anti-social behaviour outside the premises, behaviour that might annoy or anger neighbours and feed into discriminatory attitudes that others in society might hold about homeless citizens. And, there, at the bottom of the document I found the rationale I had been looking for: 'to build a society where people look out for each other, where they value each other.'

The rationale for writing this chapter is the same. Whereas the soup-kitchen manager is seeking to make his little corner of society better by encouraging respect within and across local groups, I am staking out my own little corner through discussion of what I see as key changes that need to be made if the goal of a more equal distribution of security is ever to be met. In the sections that follow, I draw upon the work of Nancy Fraser (1997) to sketch out both transformative and affirmative steps that can and should be taken.

In her highly influential work on the pursuit of social justice within contemporary societies, Fraser (1997) argues that the cause of advancing social justice for marginalized groups often requires efforts aimed at both redistribution and recognition. The pairing of such efforts is necessary because injustice typically runs along both socio-economic and cultural or symbolic lines, particularly in relation to those groups that Fraser terms 'bivalent' (ibid.: 20). Using the categories of 'gender' and 'race' to illustrate her point, she suggests that bivalent collectives are differentiated from other collectivities 'by virtue of both the political-economic structure and the cultural-valuational structure of society. When oppressed or subordinated, they therefore suffer injustices that are traceable to both political economy and culture simultaneously' (ibid.: 19). As Fraser further explains, both forms of injustice 'are rooted in processes and practices that systematically disadvantage some groups of people vis-à-vis others. Both, consequently, should be remedied' (ibid.: 19). Below, I argue that success at the task of equalizing security across society requires affirmative and transformative practices that must, of necessity, also lead to the recognition of the homeless citizen *as a citizen* in the fullest sense.

Building Recognition

They are looked upon by the general public as being bums; they don't want to work, they don't want to do anything, all they want to do is stand on the corner and beg for money, so they're asking for whatever they get and whatever they get is fine with us, we don't care. In actual fact, in the majority of the people I deal with, a lot of them have suffered hard times over the years. A lot of them have mental health issues ... a lot of them have fallen through the cracks.

– Police officer, Toronto

To say that homeless citizens are among the most stigmatized of social groups is to say something so obvious and so well known that it is highly unlikely to occasion any particular sense of surprise on the part of the reader. After all, images of slum dwellers, beggars, poorhouse residents, paupers, and other destitute individuals have long filled the public imaginary, and, with few deviations, such people have tended to be seen as bearing a tainted social status that marks them as deserving objects of public scorn and punitive treatment. Indeed, we can even turn to historical records to see how the poor of the Middle Ages were often subject to repressive, stigmatizing laws aimed at their social control (Chambliss 1964). As Jo Phelan and colleagues note (1997: 323), through the enactment of poor laws in England and the United States,

> destitute persons were separated from society and were relegated to workhouses (which were sometimes combined with jails), in which rights of citizenship were withdrawn, families were separated, and work was difficult and demeaning ... Many of these policies were clearly intended to stigmatize. For example, those receiving public assistance were required to wear distinctive clothing and badges ... which were 'rightly ordered to be fix'd as some public Marks of Shame' (Alcock 1752: 17). Harsh policies and social ostracism were accompanied by negative attitudes toward public relief and a tendency to blame poor people for their situation.

Despite a 'war on poverty,' and a brief trend towards the end of the 1980s when homelessness was seen as a social problem worthy of a public response, in many places public attitudes towards poverty have shifted little over the centuries. Surveying the social landscape in the United States, T. Knecht and L. Martinez (2009: 291) note that public opinion generally holds that the homeless citizen is 'work averse, filthy, and worthy of our contempt.' Stigmatizing social attitudes are helped along in this regard by ideologies that treat both economic success and failure as solely the result of individual efforts rather than the end products of various social factors and, in some cases, misfortunes brought about by the vicissitudes of life. To be poor in capitalist societies is to be morally suspect. But those who are homeless are more than poor: by the very nature of the interlocking social problems that create and sustain homelessness, the homeless citizen is stigmatized on many levels, since members of this group also frequently hold other forms of negative status, such as 'mentally ill,' 'substance abuser,' 'criminal,' or 'sexually promiscuous.'

As Fraser would put the matter, the homeless citizen is subject to 'misrecognition.' Misrecognition is a 'fundamental injustice' that entails 'social subordination in the sense of being prevented from participating as a peer in social life as a result of institutionalized patterns of cultural value that constitute one as relatively unworthy of respect or esteem' (Fraser 2008a: 59; 2008b: 84). Misrecognition makes it socially acceptable both to despise and to devalue homeless citizens. This devaluation takes the form of a range of harms that homeless individuals disproportionately suffer, including routine harassment, physical and sexual violence, demeaning stereotypes, punitive laws, and aggressive and/or discriminatory policing practices, among others. Because they are the carriers of stigmatized identities, any negative treatment that members of this group receive can be ignored, trivialized, or otherwise justified as 'just desserts.'

If we seek to equalize the distribution of security or any another public good, then it is imperative that we address and alter discriminatory social attitudes that support maldistribution. Otherwise, as we have seen with the deliberate shrinking of the social- safety net and the hardening of public attitudes, any equitable gains made are too easily subject to reversals. In arguing for transformative projects aimed at according positive recognition to those who are homeless and other stigmatized social groups, I am mindful of Fraser's (2008a) injunction that we ought to treat misrecognition as a social harm in and of itself, and not solely as a justification for redressing economic or other forms of maldistribution. While I wholeheartedly agree with her concerns on this issue, to support the aims of this book – which are more narrowly focused on questions related to the equalization of security – I am going to have to bracket out larger issues of recognition and their import for social justice. Instead, within these pages I adopt the more limited stance that recognition of marginalized groups as full partners in society is central to achieving and sustaining a more equitable distribution of security. I do so on the ground that recognizing the homeless citizen *as a full citizen* is necessary for the reasons articulated above: that their devalued social status too easily serves as a justification for our unwillingness to see and respond to the criminal threats homeless citizens face and the victimization they routinely experience.

How can we begin the process of according positive recognition to the homeless citizen? Fraser (2008: 84) suggests that the only viable means of overcoming the injustices of misrecognition 'is to replace institutionalized cultural patterns that subordinate people with patterns that establish them as peers.' To do so requires a deconstructive politics that moves people away from seeing the world in simple binaries – good/ bad, black/white, poor/not poor – and therefore destabilizes hierarchical social identities. Ultimately, social justice for the homeless citizen requires such efforts, and anything that falls short of this mark will likely achieve little. Half-gap measures will fail because, again, 'homeless' is not a single status based on one stigmatized social identity – 'poor' – but on multiple layers of stigmatized identities. Thus, it is not a question of reclaiming one devalued social identity, but learning to value and respect all. For this reason, positive portrayals of homeless individuals on television, or efforts to reclaim words such as 'bum,' while perhaps offering some potential for positive consequences, are just not going to do the trick. This is a seriously complex problem and one that, as we have seen in relation to the struggles of other oppressed groups, requires more radical solutions.

Redistributing Security

They are the weaker people in society, they need protection. They don't really have a voice.

– Service provider, Toronto

It is important to recognize from the outset that the best means of ensuring a more equal access to security and other public goods is through transformative efforts aimed at 'deep redistribution' – that is, through restructuring of institutional and cultural practices that support maldistribution. However, while deep redistribution will resolve various social problems identified in this book and elsewhere, I am not nearly optimistic enough to suggest that such a radical shift can be treated as anything but a long-range goal at best. Indeed, given the present political and economic climate, it is unlikely that public attitudes and policies towards the homeless and other marginalized citizens will shift without sustained, protracted struggle. To be clear: it is not my view that we ought not to fight *now* for the implementation of progressive, socially inclusive policies that will fundamentally restructure class/gender/race and other relations and to resist those political agendas that would lead to further marginalization; rather, it is my belief that pushing for such structural changes will, in the current political climate, meet with significant resistance that may take years, if not decades, to overcome. Thus, I conceive of the transformative shifts I have described above as long-term goals. In doing so, I am seeking to be pragmatic about what can realistically be accomplished in the short term, and what will likely entail significant levels of campaigning.

Meanwhile, in the short term, problems remain that in good conscience we must admit require immediate attention. Among these is the plight of homeless citizens generally, and, in particular, their greater exposure to criminal harm, which is linked to an inability to access security. While we work towards deep redistribution, we can and should also attempt to achieve greater security for these citizens and similarly situated others through affirmative projects aimed at increasing security and alleviating suffering and fears. In this section I want to sketch out in general terms how such affirmative projects can best be achieved, saving discussion of practical suggestions for the next section.

First, I should begin by acknowledging that I share the conviction of I. Loader and N. Walker (2007: 7) that, when it comes to facilitating access to security, the 'democratic state has a necessary and virtuous role to play' (see also Zedner 2009; Bayley and Shearing 1996). My quibble is thus not with the nature of the original bargain, but with the extent to which the promise of state-based security for all citizens remains unfulfilled. As much as the state has frequently proven to be inept or even unwilling to foster wider distribution of this public good, at present it still remains the best means of potentially equalizing access. With the various forms of capital at its disposal – economic, symbolic, legal, political – the state cumulatively has more resources than any other single social agent and thus is best positioned to effect important social change in this area. The state is also best positioned to effect many, if not all, of the intermediate steps – some of which are outlined below – that can be taken to increase individual and collective security within marginalized communities.

A similar consideration is the fact that other potential actors are either inadequate to the task of fostering equal distribution of security, or uninterested for reasons of self-interest. In relation to the latter, certainly the commercial marketplace – which is too easily offered up as the solution to all ills within American neo-liberal rhetoric – has no interest in securing those who lack the means to consume their products and services. Instead, private security markets offer an exclusive good that is seen as desirable *precisely because it is exclusive* (Crawford 2006; Hope 2000). In relation to the former, as Steve Herbert (2006) notes, communities that are poor and struggling under the burden of multiple social ills are often too 'unbearably light' to withstand the weight of ongoing security projects, without significant investment in infrastructure, people, and resources in both the start-up phase and over the long haul (see also Huey and Quirouette 2010).

One Step: Shifting Public Policy

In the preceding section I argued that the state – by virtue of its mandated role as *the* source of security among citizens and its abundant access to the resources necessary to facilitating its distribution – must retain its primary role and function in this area. This is not to say, however, that average citizens cannot also play a significant part in efforts aimed at the redistribution of security. They can and they do. A liberal state is, after all, both responsible to its citizens and a reflection of the desires of the majority of those citizens. Thus, as I have argued elsewhere in relation to public policing, citizens tend to get the style of governance that they want and/or are for which they are willing to mobilize (Huey 2007). If citizens want changes in public policy – by which I mean changes that lead to greater equality of access to security – then we can begin by mobilizing for pro-social domestic policies at all levels of government, as well as against public policies that increase marginalization and other forms of social harm.

For one thing, all citizens can mobilize against economic and social policies that will have the effect of producing greater numbers of homeless citizens. As an example, in the current economic climate we can see the disastrous effects of harsh public-welfare rules and limits. Intended as a sop to the popular but mistaken view that 'welfare queens' and other public demons are abusing taxpayers' dollars, rules strictly circumscribing welfare eligibility have had the effect of creating great stress and hardship for many of those citizens who were only barely hanging on financially before the economic crash of 2008. With limited public support available for those now in need, we find people living in cars, families temporarily housed in motels, and others torn apart because parents are unable to find the money to pay for even the cheapest of hotels to keep their families together. The uninsured and the under-insured, notably in the United States, have been pushed into debt and are facing homelessness as a result of exorbitant medical bills that they will likely never be able to pay. In some parts of the United States, medical facilities that offered oncology and other vital medical treatments to the poor are closing because of a lack of funding, forcing the working poor and the destitute alike to make grim choices. Concerned citizens need to fight against public policy that creates or exacerbates these conditions.

Citizens can also choose to vote against measures that will further disadvantage homeless citizens and others who are already marginalized. If the preceding chapters have illustrated anything, it is that those with the fewest resources are the most vulnerable to victimization, so punitive welfare, housing, or other government policies do little more than increase vulnerability by driving the desperate into risky and/or harmful situations. In particular, citizens can resist policies that criminalize homeless citizens, particularly in relation to status offences. Cycling homeless citizens in and out jail for petty, non-harmful offences is a ridiculous waste of resources that accomplishes little more than feeding a non-productive punitive urge. The policing, court, and jail costs associated with arresting homeless people for non-payment of fines for such 'crimes' as public camping and loitering would be better spent on permanent housing, treatment beds, and improved access to medical and other services for both the homeless citizen and those at risk of homelessness. I would also argue, as scores of others do, that we should shift our thinking – and vote accordingly – with respect to current drug and prostitution policies that do little more than criminalize vulnerable people and increase their individual risk of harm.

A Few More Concrete Ideas

I want now to move even further away from more abstract discussions of the equalization of security, identifying some practical means by which the security of homeless citizens could potentially be increased in the here and now. To reiterate, my suggestions are intended only as intermediate, affirmative steps to alleviating problems of unequal access, not as cure-all solutions to the larger issues that sustain misrecognition and maldistribution.

Secure and Affordable Housing

Since homelessness itself is a major risk factor for criminal victimization, it should be of little surprise to discover that secure housing can play a significant role in reducing rates of victimization (Kushel et al. 2003; Nyamathi, Leake, and Gelberg 2000; Lam and Rosenheck 1998). Thus, at the top of any list of recommendations for increasing physical security for the homeless citizen has to be the provision of secure, affordable housing.

Investing in housing stock means more than erecting another low-income building, having a ribbon-cutting ceremony, and walking away. It entails guaranteeing that every single citizen has access to permanent housing and that temporary shelters are only ever used as short-term measures rather than as ongoing or permanent solutions. It also means diversifying the existing housing stock to create a variety of spaces for individuals with different issues, including those deemed 'hard to house' because of active addictions and/or mental illness. It further means checking the existing housing stock in poor communities on a regular basis to ensure that buildings meet minimum regulatory standards. As someone who has seen inside some fairly horrific accommodations – spaces that appear to lack decent sanitation, adequate electrical wiring, and fire escapes – it is apparent to me that there is a lot of substandard housing stock that needs to be replaced. Buildings that are not only unsafe but also insecure, because hotel owners and staff are permitting drug dealing and violent criminal activities to occur on premises, need to be shut down in order to increase the security of tenants. I have heard too many stories over the years of drug dealers trying to hide out in people's hotel rooms to evade police, or of people being threatened in their homes by individuals looking for money or drugs, to be overly sympathetic to the business needs of drug dealers.

We know that some homelessness is created through the activities of hotel owners who defraud social-assistance housing programs by collecting multiple cheques for the same room, leaving some aid recipients without a roof. A source of major frustration for community groups and police is the perceived unwillingness of government agencies to investigate and charge those owners engaging in fraudulent activities. This situation needs to remedied through site inspections of hotels and other enforcement measures.

Rental tenancy regulations in many jurisdictions also need to be strengthened to protect the rights of renters, so that individuals cannot be unjustly unhoused. Landlords should be encouraged to permit renters to keep a pet. Indeed, for some homeless citizens, the inability to secure housing that would allow them to keep a beloved dog or cat can be a major barrier to getting off the street. For others, the loss of a pet to acquire a roof is not only emotionally devastating but a source of insecurity. A woman who lives in a SRO hotel in Vancouver and was forced to give up her dog explains why this issue is important: 'There also needs to be a real Tenancy Act that does not discriminate against responsible dog owners, because we need to be able to keep our dogs. When a landlord tells anybody in the Downtown Eastside they can't keep their dog, then I feel that that should make the landlord liable for any theft and of course any danger that happens to you on the street. That never happened when I had a dog. They made me give up my dog. She was my best protector.'

Capacity Building in Poorer Communities

Among the lessons learned from the repeated failure of community-policing initiatives in marginalized neighbourhoods is that such communities are often ill-equipped to take on the burden of generating or sustaining internal security without significant state support and investment (Bayley and Shearing 1996; Johnston and Shearing 2003; Herbert 2007). One answer to the security problem must therefore entail sustained state-based investment in local capacity-building projects that provide the internal infrastructure to deal not only with the social issues plaguing a given community but also the insecurity these issues can create. In other words, governments need not only to increase funding to poorer communities but also to begin to require local recipients of government grant programs to plan for and address foreseeable security issues related to the subject of an application. Thus, if an application is brought forward to fund a bottle depot or a needle exchange, means of dealing with security issues related to the operation of the facility must be a critical component of the plan and be funded accordingly. To encourage local groups to think about and plan for site security and the security of their client groups, those grant applications that include a security component could be weighted more favourably in the rank ordering of applicants in the pool. To ensure public accountability and, in particular, that funds are being used for both their primary and security purposes, government granting agencies should be required to conduct site visits and follow-ups with local groups and their clients.

Another means by which security can be generated through state investment is offered by L. Johnston and C. Shearing (2003) in their own analysis of security maldistribution. These authors prescribe a mixed-market-based approach in which local communities utilize public funds – in the form of block grants – to purchase public, private, and mixed public-private forms of security. Such an approach, they suggest, 'could help to iron out inequities; it could lead to the development of security regimes appropriate to the needs of particular communities; and it could invest direct authority in the hands of those most affected by existing inequities' (ibid.: 144). While this could lead to an even greater opting out of public services – a fear often articulated in relation to the purchase of private security by wealthier communities – it is likely that the public police would resist the diminution of their role (Stenson 1993), which could, in turn, generate a positive change in how they police poorer communities. In this context, perhaps the market *may* offer a solution, but only through the willingness of governments to provide public funding of a diverse array of policing options.

Improved Oversight of Both Public and Private Security Actors

Both the public system of security and the private market can be viable options, however, only if the people being policed have confidence in the fairness of the systems used – that is, if they believe that using those systems is preferable to alternatives because their use will lead to just outcomes. At present, and to a significant degree, that is not the case with the public police. In each of the studies I have conducted over the years, for every individual who said that they would report a crime to the police, there were many others who stated that they were afraid of police, thought they might find themselves arrested, and had little faith that police officers would take their complaint, investigate, and so on. In other words, as we know, there are a fair number of homeless citizens who do not see the police as representing a society to which they belong, or as offering a service to which they are entitled and will receive simply by virtue of citizenship. To change such attitudes requires a genuine effort on the part of police organizations to be more accountable to each of the local publics they serve, and not solely or largely those with the loudest voices or largest wallets.

One way in which police accountability could be improved upon is through changes to police complaint systems. For example, the individual in the previous chapter who did not have his report of an assault by a private security guard taken seriously by the attending police officer has grounds for a complaint against the police officer. To facilitate such reports, public education about the complaints process needs to reach all communities, and reporting mechanisms to be made more accessible for communities that lack easy access to phones or the Internet. Further, since complainants have had one or more negative experiences with police, they may be unwilling to attend a police station to report in person. One viable solution might be to utilize third-party reporting systems, where reports are taken by trusted service providers (such programs are discussed in further detail below). Another option might be, for those organizations that operate storefront community-policing centres (CPCs) with paid civilians and volunteers, to have reports taken within the community at a CPC by a designated civilian staff member.

When the issue of police complaints is discussed in some communities, concerns also arise as to whether investigations are conducted externally or by officers within the same agency. In relation to the latter, changes need to be made to ensure public confidence and to avoid the charge of 'why bother? It's just police investigating themselves.' To address these issues, some jurisdictions have police complaints investigated by other police agencies, or by civilian-oversight committees.

The man who was assaulted by the security guard also has grounds for a complaint against the guard. Unfortunately, in most jurisdictions state regulations governing private security are so loose as to be lamentable. In cases involving unlicensed security, often the only recourse available is to call or write a letter of complaint to the employer or the business contracting the service, who are under no obligation to respond. With respect to security actors licensed by the state, mechanisms are often in place that allow for complaints to be filed with a government office. However, the institution of such processes does not necessarily represent a significant improvement. In one province I studied, the legislation did not allow for complainants to be advised as to the disposition of a case after the investigation was completed; thus, they never knew if their complaint was dismissed as unfounded or if any further action was taken (Huey, Ericson, and Haggerty 2007). Regardless of whether the actors within the private market ever become agents who can decrease the security gap faced by homeless and other marginalized citizens, regulations governing the use of private security need to be strengthened for the good of all citizens.

Developing Police Outreach and Local Reporting Programs

Increasing public accountability is only part of the equation when it comes to the matter of improving relations between public police and homeless citizens, and thereby increasing the potential for the latter to access security through the former. As I discussed in chapter 3, when homeless citizens are queried about their attitudes to reporting crime to the police, previous negative experiences frequently inhibit reporting. Conversely, positive relations with an individual officer increase trust in that person and the likelihood that a victim will come forward to tell their story to a police officer they know and trust (see also Huey 2007 and Huey and Quirouette 2009). Thus, one means of strengthening police ties to the local community, and addressing local crime issues that plague the community, is through police outreach programs that encourage officers to spend a portion of their routine patrol activity simply sitting down and getting to know people and groups in their assigned neighbourhoods. By people and groups, I do not mean local business owners or other pro-police factions. As we have seen too often in the research on community policing, there is a tendency on the part of police agencies to focus their efforts on working with community factions from which they already draw support (Huey 2007; Saunders 1999). Instead of practising 'business as usual' under the guise of 'community policing,' I am talking about taking the novel approach of treating all citizens within a neighbourhood as the constituency that the police are mandated to serve, and seeing value in learning about who they are and what their life experiences have been. Such an approach is the perhaps the best means of fostering individual trust in the police.

In relation to the problem of the 'anti-snitching prohibition,' which represents a significant barrier to crime reporting within homeless and other marginalized communities, I have written elsewhere on the merits of third-party reporting programs that facilitate anonymous reporting (Huey and Quirouette 2009, 2010a, b). In essence, what these programs permit is a means through which frightened victims can come forward to trusted service providers participating in the program and tell their stories anonymously. The victim is then afforded the opportunity to decide whether they want the report forwarded to police to be treated as 'information only' or to be investigated (a process in which the victim consents to participate). Not only do such programs offer a means of avoiding the social exclusion, harassment, and/or violence that can follow discovery of police reporting, at least one program studied in Edinburgh also has an informal policy in place to limit the possibility of victims who come forward being arrested for outstanding warrants.[2] Until such time as police are able to work through the cultural barriers that separate them from the homeless, the encouraging of reporting through safer, alternative methods represents one of the best potential means for them to address criminal threats facing community members.

Crime-Prevention Counselling and Anti-Violence Education

During interviews with shelter workers and homeless women in Montreal about the issues the latter face while trying to stay safe on the streets, it was not uncommon for respondents to say that what they needed was self-defence classes. Of the few women encountered who had had such training, they tended to state that they felt safer and were either better prepared to defend themselves from an attacker or had already done so. Although a self-defence component would be very useful, given the wide scope of victimization that homeless citizens face, I would suggest that what is required more is crime-prevention counselling, and, in particular, counselling that deals with both the prevention of and the available responses to various forms of victimization. Such counselling, which needs to be part of an ongoing effort within communities, would be a worthwhile investment in both time and resources for local governments, police, and community-service organizations, as well as providing innumerable potential benefits for citizens.

What is also required within homeless communities is education aimed at reducing intimate partner violence and violence within families. There are still far too many individuals who are being stalked, harassed, and physically abused and/or nearly killed by partners and former partners. Whether as part of ongoing crime-prevention counselling efforts or as a separate program organized within communities, anti-violence education needs to be a significant component of any crime-prevention initiatives aimed at equalizing security.

Victimization Services

A disturbing fact I have repeatedly encountered within my own research is that not only do victims often not report their experiences to police or other authorities, but for various reasons they often fail to seek out seek medical, psychological, or other services post-victimization or to continue prescribed treatments (Stermac and Paradis 2001; Padgett et al. 2006). For instance, J. Jasinski et al. (2005) found that 44 per cent of women interviewed in their U.S. sample stated that they had received a 'serious injury' from being criminally victimized, and 30.8 per cent categorized their injury as 'somewhat serious.' However, 43.6 per cent of women victimized stated that they had received no medical treatment and 58.5 per cent had not spoken with a psychologist, social worker, or mental-health professional about their experience(s) (ibid.). Failure to receive appropriate medical and counselling services after experiencing the trauma of violent victimization has repeatedly been shown to have significant negative mental and physical health implications for victims, as well as increasing the odds that homeless crime victims will experience further victimization (North et al. 1994; Stewart et al. 2004; Whitbeck et al. 2007; D'Ercole and Struening 1996; Tucker et al. 2005; Ambrosio et al. 1992).

The reasons for failures to seek services post-victimization are varied. For some, fear that seeking medical or other assistance will lead to a police report inhibits help-seeking, since retaliatory violence for 'snitching' remains a significant concern (Huey and Quirouette 2010). For others, attending counselling or treatment sessions invokes anxiety and dread, for it means leaving safe spaces to enter into potentially threatening territory and coming into contact with potentially threatening people (Padgett et al. 2006). And, most obviously, many lack the financial means to travel to other neighbourhoods to attend programs, while others, in their list of daily priorities, place treatment behind finding food or a bed for the night.

If we are serious about increasing security for the homeless citizen, we need to establish spaces that offer a range of victim services within one building. Such spaces need to be conveniently located and easily accessible, and they should operate on a drop-in basis rather than on an appointment-based scheduling system.[3] Excepting rare circumstances involving minors and/or an immediate threat of death, we also need to make sure that victims know that the services they access are completely confidential and that treatment is decoupled from law-enforcement activities.

Access to Phones

In the previous chapter, I related the story of a woman living in a SRO hotel in Vancouver without access to a phone. As may be recalled, she was too afraid to leave her hotel room to locate a phone and call the police to report an abduction she had witnessed from her window. Although it is the case that some homeless citizens do own cell-phones and utilize pay-as-you-go plans, the majority do not. Nor is there always unfettered access to phones within many shelters, and SRO hotels rarely, if ever, provide phones in rooms. As someone who utilizes public pay-phones, I can speak knowledgeably about the fact that too often they are out of service.

If we want to encourage crime reporting to police, then providing accessible phone services is a must. One option that was floated in Vancouver's DTES for women in the sex trade was the provision of pre-programmed cell-phones that would permit free emergency calls to 9–1–1 only. In a similar vein, agreements could be put in place with public-payphone service providers to ensure regular repair and maintenance, as well the installation of phones that permit free calls to be made to pre-programmed emergency numbers. Access to public phones in common areas of buildings and shelters housing homeless citizens also needs to be facilitated.

A Dark Future

The harshest sentence is to leave people without support on the street.
– Police officer, Vancouver

Thus far I have been offering both simple and more complex solutions to the problem of insecurity among those who lack the means to make up for the deficit in security with which they are faced as a result of their socio-economic status. Now I wish to focus on the very real likelihood that this gap will increase to even more dangerous levels as a result of the continuation of the political, social, and economic trends discussed in the first chapter.

At the time of writing this book, various nations are experiencing ongoing economic instability as a result of the major financial crisis of 2008, a crisis that is directly attributable to laissez-faire economic policies. Such an attribution is easy to make, since all of the hallmarks of the American variant of neo-liberal economic thought can be identified as contributing factors to the creation of the crisis, from unrestrained market forces and deregulation to high-risk speculation and predatory lending practices. What makes this situation so infuriating for many critics of American neo-liberalism is that, long before the crash, there were sufficient warning signs that what appeared to be economic growth was really a series of market-induced bubbles generating little more than increasing levels of income disparity and economic uncertainty.

Now, with a largely preventable recession upon us, significant job losses across economic sectors have pushed many individuals and families around the globe into unemployment, as well as into becoming homeless or at serious risk of homelessness. Ironically, given that Americans have been fed a steady diet of positive messages on the joys of trickle-down economics, the situation appears particularly bleak in the United States. Recently, the National Alliance to End Homelessness (2011) reported that, from 2008 to 2009, 'conditions worsened among all four economic indicators examined ... [from] housing affordability for poor people, unemployment, poor workers' income, and foreclosure status.' As a result, during this same period 'the number of unemployed people in America increased by 60 percent from 8.9 to 14.3 million' (ibid.).

While Canada's unemployment rate is said to be recovering, as is often the case, increases in employment rates can be attributed to the creation of growing numbers of part-time jobs. Further, Canada has its own significant problems with respect to homelessness: in 2011 the Canadian federal government estimated that there are 150,000 to 300,000 people who are 'living in shelters or on the streets' (HRSDC 2011). Many of these citizens are 'single women and lone-parent families headed by women,' and 'families with children living in poverty, street youth, Aboriginal persons, persons with mental illness, the working poor, and new immigrants are disproportionately reflected in the homeless population' (ibid.).

The U.K. unemployment rate, while hovering slightly above its forty-year national average of 7.22 at 7.8 per cent, also remains below that of the United States (U.K. Office for National Statistics 2011). However, various indicators – including the fact that 1.45 million people in the United Kingdom are currently claiming Job Seeker's Allowance – suggest that all is not well (ibid.). For instance, national housing statistics released in December 2010 reveal that the situation for homeless and at-risk groups is no better in the United Kingdom: in its quarterly analysis of housing under the U.K.'s statutory housing bill, local councils in England report that, although the numbers of citizens in temporary accommodations decreased slightly, the numbers of individuals and families applying for housing are on the increase (by 11 per cent), as are the number of individuals accepted for housing (12 per cent) (Thompson 2010). These increases, which can be attributed to slow economic recovery, mark a significant change over the declining numbers posted in earlier quarters (ibid.).

Given the apparent inability of American-style neo-liberal policies to generate the much-vaunted rising tide that 'lifts all boats' – or even many boats beyond a privileged few – it is worrying that we are observing the unchecked continuation of neo-liberal policy trends across various countries (see also Harvey 2011). If there was ever a time to see the social-safety net expanding rather than contracting, that time would appear to be now. Instead, we see little change. To illustrate this point, we need look no further than the failure of the Barack Obama administration to implement meaningful health-care reform in the United States at a time when millions of citizens are without basic health care. The inability of the United States to realize significant change on this issue represents nothing more than the unwillingness of policy makers, vested interests, and, indeed, many citizens to shift course towards a much-needed expansion of the welfare state.

In response to the economic crisis, Canadians, too, hardly seem to be on the verge of embracing a renaissance of Keynesian welfarism. In 2011 Canadians elected a majority Conservative government that has consistently run on Canadian-style neo-liberal economic policies coupled with a populist 'tough on crime' stance. As depressing as it is to contemplate, it is not unreasonable to expect that this new government will mirror earlier ones that have cut provincial transfer payments, resulting in decreases to the funding of areas that benefit lower-income Canadians (Gaetz 2010). Times are also scary in the United Kingdom, as a coalition government there has made drastic cuts to vital spending areas, including the formerly untouchable area of higher education. In relation to homelessness, in April 2011 the U.K government announced significant cuts to housing benefits, which will very likely push many families and individuals into the streets (Morphy 2011). This announcement came on the heels of an earlier proposed regulatory change that, if passed, could result in some 88,000 young people being denied housing benefits (ibid.).

It does not take a crystal ball to foresee that, if left unchecked, current economic and social policies that create, exacerbate, punish, and maintain homelessness will have devastating effects on an ever-increasing number of citizens. After all, we will be increasing the numbers of those citizens left homeless at a time when we are cutting services that would lift them out of this condition. We would be, in the words of the police officer quoted above, sentencing individuals and families to the harshest of sentences: being on the street without support. The tragedy is compounded by the fact that such increases are occurring at a time when we are already not doing nearly enough to assist our existing homeless citizens, who, as I have demonstrated in the preceding chapters, suffer disproportionately from criminal victimization among other devastating problems. Their plight, and the plight of those growing numbers of people who will become homeless in the future, calls for an effective response. We should be taking steps not only to reduce, indeed eradicate, homelessness but also to enforce the obligation of the state to secure all its citizens.

What will the future look like if we do not begin the process of recognizing all of our citizens as citizens and providing assistance to ensure that they are secure, healthy, and able to participate fully in civic life? As their numbers increase and they are increasingly denied assistance to rise out of poverty, or even the opportunity to access the most basic of services as resources and empathy grow increasingly scarce, the security gap illustrated throughout this book will all too likely become an unbridgeable chasm. If we want to know what such chasms look like, we need only turn our attention to the favelas of Brazil or the slums of Mumbai.

A Final Thought

We need to protect each citizen.
                                                    – Service provider, Edinburgh

In a recent summation of the state of security and security politics, Lucia Zedner (2009: 164) argued that changing patterns of security distribution have left us with the 'problem of how to achieve equitable distribution of this basic public good,' a problem that 'is one of the most important issues of contemporary criminal justice.' I could not agree more. While some scholars have contended that the only viable solution to the security dilemmas we face is to jettison the idea of security as a desirable or necessary state of being, I argue that such an approach is equivalent to throwing the baby out with the bathwater. To put the matter even more succinctly, the problem of chronic insecurity faced by millions of people each year is not a mere abstraction, a theoretical puzzle that can be neatly solved without taking into account the very real effects that a lack of security can have on a vulnerable population. Indeed, the very reason that I am able to enter into this debate at all is because I live in a relative state of security that affords me the luxury of giving thought and voice to such considerations. Everyone should be so fortunate.

Appendix: Research Methods

As noted in the Introduction, the data in this book are derived from interviews and fieldwork from three separate research studies that I conducted from 2000 to 2009. In this appendix, I elaborate further on those studies and my data-collection methods.

Study 1: Vancouver, Edinburgh, and San Francisco (2000–3)

The first study on homelessness that I conducted sought to explore the nature of policing in economically and socially depressed communities often referred to as 'skid rows.' Collection of the data used in this study took place between January 2000 and December 2003. Data-gathering methods included interviews, field observation, and document analysis. Eighty-six interviews were conducted with 101 interviewees. Some interviewees were identified through a preliminary study of textual materials and contacted directly. Others were identified through the use of snowball sampling.

As can be seen from the table below, five different groups of participants were recruited for this study. Since securing access to homeless citizens can be difficult – particularly in foreign cities – I sought the approval of community groups and service providers who work with homeless populations in order to access their client groups. The range of services whose workers and clients agreed to participate included shelters, soup kitchens, and day centres, as well as community groups. Patrons of these services were told in advance that I would be coming to do research on the policing of homeless populations and were asked if they wished to participate. When I arrived at the site, I would be introduced and those who chose to participate would go off with me for

Table 1 Interviews

Subject category	Edinburgh	San Francisco	Vancouver	Totals by category
Homeless citizens	14	11	7	32
Community groups/service providers	9	9	12	30
Police personnel	8	9	12	29
Local businesses	1	1	2	4
City representatives	2	2	2	6
Totals per city	34	32	35	101

a coffee or a sit-down in a private on-site location or a nearby coffee shop. Sometimes, if it was a slow day and few people were approaching me, I would go up to someone at a service facility and ask them if they would be willing to share their insights and experiences. In a few notable cases, a homeless citizen would see me conducting field research or on my way to an interview and approach me to ask what I was doing. In several instances, those conversations led to interviews.

I also interviewed staff at the facilities through which I was working. Shelter staff, soup-kitchen workers, day-centre managers, community activists, and others were asked for their perspectives on the policing of the communities within which they work. To discover how the police view their work with homeless citizens, police officers of varying ranks – from frontline officers to senior police managers – were interviewed in each of the cities studied. And, to learn more about the pressures placed on police within these communities, I gained access to both city representatives (politicians and civil servants) and local businesses.

To supplement the interview data, I conducted observational research. I began by spending a couple of days in both Edinburgh (2002) and San Francisco (2000) to scope out potential research locations, speak to homeless citizens, and make contact with service providers.[1] Subsequently, in 2003, I spent approximately one month in each of the cities conducting interviews and field observation. During that time, I spent two to three days per week, for two- to six-hour periods, at night and during the day, observing citizens and police in various spaces within my target communities. During fieldwork, notes and photographs were taken in order to document physical and social characteristics of the environment, as well as interactions within selected spaces.

Primary and secondary documents were also gathered and analysed in order to provide an understanding of some aspects of the social, political, economic, and geographical nature of each of the cities' downtown environs. Document sources varied and included both hard-copy text and web-based materials: city reports, community reports, materials of non-governmental organizations, and relevant legislation and regulations. During interviews, I was sometimes given copies of police forms and organizational reports that were subsequently used to inform my analysis. Using various databases and search engines, I also obtained relevant news articles from major and smaller news outlets in each of the cities.

Study 2: Montreal and Ottawa (2007)

During the course of conducting the first study, I noted that when several of the women interviewed spoke of victimization, they also referenced various gendered strategies they employ in order to keep safe. As a consequence of the insights they provided, I decided to explore more fully the issue of homeless women's adoption of strategies to minimize their risk of victimization. Thus, in 2007 I began a second study more narrowly focused on this issue of gender and victimization. Working with service providers in Montreal and Ottawa, Eric Berndt and I located and interviewed sixteen homeless women about issues of personal safety and criminal victimization. In keeping with the research question I developed from my previous study, each woman was asked in particular about what, if any, gendered survival strategies they employ in order to prevent victimization on the streets. In order to diversify the data I would draw upon, we also interviewed nine service providers from three different organizations in Montreal and Ottawa. Service providers whom we interviewed were asked to speak to the dangers their female clients face on the street, as well as to women's modes of adaptation.

As with the first study, our access to the homeless populations was facilitated by supportive community agencies. In Montreal, we worked through a shelter for women. In Ottawa, we gained access to clients through the auspices of a day centre and a shelter (the shelter also facilitated our access to a medical facility where we met a couple of their clients who were receiving treatment). The women who agreed to participate in this study were from a variety of ethno-cultural backgrounds,

Table 2 Interviews

Subject category	Montreal	Ottawa	Totals by category
Homeless citizens	10	6	16
Community groups/service providers	3	6	9
Totals per city	13	12	25

including Aboriginals, Latinas, anglo-Canadians, and franco-Canadians. Their ages ranged from seventeen to sixty. Some of the women we met were fairly new to the streets when interviewed; others had spent more than half their lifetime in street-based communities.

Study 3: Edinburgh, Toronto, and Vancouver

During the course of conducting research in Edinburgh in 2002 and 2003, I discovered that a couple of the city's shelters and the Lothian and Borders Police Force were jointly operating an outreach reporting program for homeless victims of crime. I then made the decision to collect interview data and written information on this program and its operation, with the idea in mind that it could potentially serve as a model program in other cities. In 2008 I returned to Edinburgh with Marianne Quirouette and began a two-phase study. In the first phase, we collected data to evaluate the strengths and limitations of the Edinburgh project, now called 'Take Control.' In the second phase, we returned to Canada and interviewed homeless citizens, community-service providers, and police about the utility of implementing a similar program in two Canadian cities: Toronto and Vancouver.

In Edinburgh, we began by interviewing representatives of each of the service organizations participating in the program. We also interviewed representatives of homelessness organizations not involved in the program – in order to discover why they were not participating and to hear their views on its potential benefits and disadvantages for their organization and, more important, for their service users – and police personnel with direct experience of the program and its operation. And, as always, we sought out the views of those most important for our research: homeless citizens. As has become a standard practice in my research, we sought access to the views, experiences, and beliefs of

Table 3 Interviews

Respondent category	Edinburgh	Toronto	Vancouver	Totals by category
Police personnel	2	12	8	22
Service providers	12	14	14	40
Homeless service users	17	22	12	51
Totals per city	31	48	34	113

homeless adults through the cooperation and facilitation of the service organizations that had agreed to participate in our study.

For our Canadian research, we developed a non-probability sample of the maximum number of homelessness service providers in Vancouver and Toronto – including shelters, soup kitchens, day centres, legal services, outreach services, and community-advocacy groups – and invited each to participate. Of these, eight organizations in Toronto and ten in Vancouver agreed to participate by allowing us access to both their staff and their clients. As with the 2003 study, clients were informed in advance of our presence and the purposes of our study, and were asked whether they wished to participate or not. Since the participating organizations work with various issues related to homelessness, we ended up with a diverse array of participants, including men, women, the transgendered, persons of colour, those with addictions and/or mental-health issues, and the un-housed as well as those making the transition to more stable accommodation.

In order to round out this study, we also sought the permission of the respective chief constables of the Vancouver and Toronto police services to interview senior command staff in each force's downtown patrol divisions, as well as frontline officers.

Notes

Introduction: The Invisible Victim

1 A more complete description of the data-collection methods used for each study can be located in the appendix that appears at the end of this book.
2 One of the issues that periodically plagues researchers on homelessness is the variability of the concept. To be clear: in each of the studies above, the term 'homeless' was defined by me to include a range of individuals who lack permanent housing, such as 'rough sleepers' (those who sleep outdoors), couch surfers, shelter users, and those who barter sex for accommodation. It also includes those citizens who are marginally housed in the often dangerous and substandard accommodations provided by Single Resident Occupancy (SROs) hotels. Of the myriad definitions of this term available, the one that I have consistently applied is perhaps closest to that of Wright (2009 [1989]: 19), who conceptualizes the state of being homeless as lacking 'regular and customary access to a conventional dwelling unit' (see also Rossi 1989).
3 More detailed information on data collection and analysis for each project can be found in Huey (2007), Huey and Berndt (2008), and Huey and Quirouette (2009) respectively.

1. Security and Citizenship

1 A small passage between two buildings, often covered.
2 While it easy to understand why I would include physical safety from criminal harm within this definition, it may be less the case with respect to property crimes. As I argue in later chapters, retaining their money and other personal belongings is seen by many homeless citizens as vital to both

their immediate safety and their sense of personal well-being. In the case of the homeless, who lack replacement insurance or the ability to absorb financial losses easily, economic victimization can mean the difference between having shelter or going without.

3 Johnston and Shearing explain the necessity of freedom from future threat in the following terms: 'Peace is more than the mere absence of present threat; it embodies the sense that one *will be* safe in the future' (2006: 5; emphasis in original).

4 Economies, as used in this sense, range from those of the individual family across various markets to that of the nation-state (Foucault 1997).

5 Elsewhere, I have demonstrated that the 'golden age of welfare' is based on the false belief that rights under social citizenship were universally granted and applied in North America in the post-war era (Huey 2007). I note that Rose (1996) makes a similar argument with respect to their application in the United Kingdom.

6 To be clear: I employ the term 'homeless citizen' throughout this book prescriptively rather than descriptively.

2. Homelessness and Criminal Victimization

1 In order to ensure the validity of their comparisons, Jasinski et al. (2010) used the same measures of victimization as those employed in the NVAWS survey.

2 A city about an hour outside Vancouver.

3 A pseudonym.

4 A pseudonym.

5 Although there have been far too few attempts to determine levels and forms of victimization experienced by homeless sexual minorities – gays, lesbians, bisexuals, and the trans-identified (GLBT) – those studies that do exist indicate that members of such groups are often singled out for harassment, intimidation, and various forms of violence because of their minority status (Cochran, Stewart, Ginzler, and Cauce 2002; Whitbeck, Chen, Hoytz, Tyler, and Johnson 2004). While these studies demonstrate that gay and bisexual youth are particularly vulnerable to physical and sexual victimization, another disturbing fact revealed by the limited research in this area is that higher rates of victimization experienced by homeless GLBT youth do not decrease as they enter into adulthood on the streets. Milburn et al. (2006) found that, whereas some forms of negative treatment experienced by homeless youth generally decrease as they adapt to their surroundings, discriminatory treatment based on sexual orientation does not dissipate.

These authors conclude that 'discrimination based on sexual orientation has a relative enduring salience' (ibid.: 669).

6 A pseudonym.
7 A pseudonym.
8 This is not an unusual story; several respondents in various cities in each of the studies referenced the practice of sexually exploiting vulnerable women and youth through drugs and alcohol.
9 Trans-identified youth and adults on the streets are particularly vulnerable to both physical and sexual assault. Indeed, one study found that trans-gendered individuals were the most likely to report having experienced both physical and sexual victimization at rates higher than those for other groups of homeless respondents surveyed (Kushel, Evans, Perry, Robertson, and Moss 2003).

3. State-Based Security

1 A pseudonym.
2 This is the informal police practice of driving a perceived 'troublemaker' to an out-of-the way spot and dumping him/her there.
3 I discuss practices related to 'dealing with it' in further detail in the next chapter.
4 As with most rules, the anti-snitching prohibition is said to permit some exceptions. Thus, despite protestations that ratting is always an action worthy of punishment, even the most dogmatic of those who affirm this prohibition state that they are willing to carve out exceptions for groups deemed uniquely vulnerable and thus in need of police protection. Generally speaking, such groups include women, children, the elderly, and the mentally ill (Huey and Quirouette 2010).

4. Self-Protection Strategies

1 The name omitted refers to a known victim of Willie Pickton; I have chosen to remove the name.
2 As with other individuals referenced in this book who are still living, this is a pseudonym.
3 Some details of the story were independently verified against other sources.
4 To be clear: while it is the case that homeless women have unequal access to material goods, many service facilities receive a wide range of clothing donations from which service users can choose. Thus, in many cases, the women interviewed had a choice as to the clothes they wore and stated in

interviews that their preferred mode of dress in the streets was male or masculine-type garb.

5 I tend to avoid questions relating to the illegal activities of respondents unless they voluntarily disclose those activities first. In many jurisdictions, carrying a concealed weapon is illegal.

5. Security through Others

1 A pseudonym.
2 A pseudonym.
3 A pseudonym.
4 Reporting to police via third parties, usually community-service providers.
5 In 2009 the city of San Francisco established a Community Justice Center for dealing with 'quality of life' and other low-level offences in the Tenderloin community. Rather than adopting a restorative-justice approach that utilizes the involvement of local community members, the new center is run like a traditional lower court with a presiding judge. While this approach gets around the problem of maintaining community participation, it is an extension of the existing criminal justice system (albeit with a kindlier face) and thus does little to address the larger problem of how to tackle the issues that lead to individual and collective insecurity within the community.

6. Security and the Homeless Citizen

1 A study by researchers Perron et al. (2008: 1478) found that, among homeless crime victims surveyed, those who had experienced physical victimization were more likely to say that they did not feel safe, whereas victims of non-physical crimes had higher levels of perceived safety. The study's authors offer an explanation for this discrepancy: 'One possibility is that persons living on the streets experience non-physical victimization as a routine part of life on the streets.'

7. Equalizing Security

1 I am choosing not to cite the document here, in order to preserve the identity of this informant.
2 In 2003 I was told by police and participating service providers that officers working in the program would exercise discretion about outstanding warrants, arresting victims only in cases where the charges are of a serious

nature (Huey 2008). In 2008 we were told that this is still the case, although the 'policy' remains 'unofficial' (Huey and Quirouette 2009).

3 There are a number of homeless citizens who organize their lives not around clocks and calendars but rather around immediate needs. Thus, an appointment-based system of accessing services simply will not work for these people.

Appendix: Research Methods

1 An initial field visit was unnecessary in Vancouver because I had already been conducting research there on related topics (see Huey, Haggerty, and Ericson 2005).

References

Akerstrom, M. (1988). 'Snitches on Snitching.' *Society*, 26(1): 22–6.

Alder, C., and D. Sandor. (1989). *Homeless Youth as Victims of Violence* (a report of the Criminology Council of Canberra). Melbourne: University of Melbourne.

Ambrosio, E., D. Baker, C. Crowe, and K. Hardill. (1992). 'The Street Health Report: A Study of the Health Status and Barriers to Health Care of Homeless Women and Men in the City of Toronto' [n.p., n.d.]. 1–79.

Anderson, E. (1999). *Code of the Street: Decency, Violence, and the Moral Life of the Inner City.* New York: W.W. Norton.

Anderson, R. (1996). 'Homeless Violence and the Informal Rules of Street Life.' *Journal of Social Distress and the Homeless*, 5(4): 369–80.

Arendt, H. (2000 [1951]). 'The Perplexities of the Rights of Man.' In P. Baehr, ed., *The Portable Hannah Arendt*. London: Penguin. 31–45.

Arnold, K. (2004). *Homelessness, Citizenship and Identity: The Uncanniness of Late Modernity.* Albany, N.Y.: SUNY Press.

Ballintyne, S. (1999). *Unsafe Streets: Street Homelessness and Crime.* London: Institute for Public Policy Research.

Bauman, Z. (2007). 'Collateral Casualties of Consumerism.' *Journal of Consumer Culture*, 7(1): 25–56.

– (2006). *Liquid Fear.* Cambridge, Mass.: Polity.

Bayley, D., and C. Shearing. (1996). 'The Future of Policing.' *Law and Society Review,* 30(3): 585–606.

Beckett, K., and S. Herbert. (2010). *Banished: The New Social Control in Urban America.* Oxford, U.K.: Oxford University Press.

Bittner, E. (1990 [1970]). *Aspects of Police Work.* Ann Arbor, Mich..: Northeastern University Press.

Black, D. (1973). 'The Mobilization of Law.' *Journal of Legal Studies* 2(1): 125–49.

Borchard, K. (2005). *The Word on the Street: Homeless Men in Las Vegas*. Las Vegas: University of Nevada Press.

Buhrich, N., T. Hodder, and M. Teesson. (2000). 'Lifetime Prevalence of Trauma among Homeless People in Sydney.' *Australian and New Zealand Journal of Psychiatry*, 34(7): 963–66.

Chambliss, W. (1964). 'A Sociological Analysis of the Laws of Vagrancy.' *Social Problems*, 12(1): 67–77.

Cheung, A., and S. Hwang. (2004). 'Risk of Death among Homeless Women: A Cohort Study and Review of the Literature.' *Canadian Medical Association Journal*, 170(8): 1243–7.

Christie, N. (2004). *A Suitable Amount of Crime*. London: Routledge.

Cochrane, B., A. Stewart, J. Ginzler, and A. Cauce. (2002). 'Challenges Faced by Homeless Sexual Minorities: Comparison of Gay, Lesbian, Bisexual, and Transgender Homeless Adolescents with their Heterosexual Counterparts.' *American Journal of Public Health*, 92(5): 773–7.

Coston, C. (2004). 'Worries about Crime: Rank-Ordering Survival Concerns among Urban Transient Females.' In C. Coston, ed., *Victimizing Vulnerable Groups: Images of Uniquely High-Risk Crime Targets*. Westport, Conn.: Greenwood. 25–35.

– (1992). 'The Influence of Race in Urban Homeless Females' Fear of Crime.' *Justice Quarterly*, 9(4): 721–6.

Coston, C., and J. Finckenauer. (2004). 'Fear of Crime among Vulnerable Populations: Homeless Women.' In C. Coston, ed., *Victimizing Vulnerable Groups: Images of Uniquely High-Risk Crime Targets*. Westport, Conn.: Greenwood. 3–24.

Crawford, A. (2006). 'Policing and Security as "Club Goods": The New Enclosures.' In J. Wood and B. Dupont, eds., *Democracy, Society and the Governance of Security*. Cambridge: Cambridge University Press. 111–38.

Davis R., and N. Henderson. (2003). 'Willingness to Report Crimes: The Role of Ethnic Group Membership and Community Efficacy.' *Crime and Delinquency*, 49(4): 564–80.

D'Ercole A., and E. Struening. (1990). 'Victimization among Homeless Women: Implications for Service Delivery.' *Journal of Community Psychology*, 18(2): 141–52.

Dietz, T., and J. Wright. (2005). 'Victimization of the Elderly Homeless.' *Care Management Journals*, 6(1): 15–21.

Dupont, B. (2006). 'Power Struggles in the Field of Security: Implications for Democratic Transformation.' In B. Dupont and J. Wood, eds., *Democracy, Society and the Governance of Security*. Cambridge: Cambridge University Press. 86–110.

– (2004). 'Security in the Age of Networks.' *Policing and Society*, 14(1): 76–91.

Ellwood, D. (1988). *Poor Support: Poverty in the American Family*. New York: Basic Books.

Ericson, R. (2007). *Crime in an Insecure World*. Cambridge: Polity.

Ericson, R., D. Barry, and A. Doyle. (2000). 'The Moral Hazards of Neo-Liberalism: Lessons from the Private Insurance Industry.' *Economy and Society*, 29(4): 532–58.

Ericson, R., and K. Haggerty. (1997). *Policing the Risk Society*. Toronto: University of Toronto Press.

Evans, K., P. Fraser, and S. Walklate. (1996). 'Whom Can You Trust? The Politics of Grassing on an Inner City Housing Estate.' *Sociological Review*, 44(3): 361–80.

Evans, R., and C. Forsyth. (2004). 'Risk Factors, Endurance of Victimization and Survival Strategies: The Impact of the Structural Location of Men and Women on the Experiences within Homeless Milieus.' *Sociological Spectrum*, 24: 79–505.

Feldman, L. (2004). *Citizens without Shelter: Homelessness, Democracy and Political Exclusion*. Ithaca, N.Y.: Cornell University Press.

Fischer, P. (2004). 'Criminal Activity and Policing.' In D. Levinson, ed., *Encyclopedia of Homelessness*. London: Sage. 91–101.

Fitzpatrick, K., M. La Gory, and F. Ritchey. (1993). 'Criminal Victimization among the Homeless.' *Justice Quarterly*, 10(3): 353–68.

Foucault, M. (2008). *The Birth of Biopolitics: Lectures at the College de France, 1978–1979*. Trans. G. Burchell. New York: Picador.

– (2003). *Society Must Be Defended: Lectures at the College de France, 1975–1976*. Ed. Mauro Bertani and Allessandro Fontana; trans. David Macey. New York: Picador.

– (1995 [1977]). *Discipline and Punish: The Birth of the Prison*. Trans. Alàn Sheridan. New York: Vintage Books.

– (1984). 'Space, Knowledge and Power.' In P. Rabinow, ed., *The Foucault Reader*. New York: Random House. 239–56.

Fraser, N. (2008a). 'Heterosexisms, Misrecognition, and Capitalism: A Response to Judith Butler.' In K. Olson, ed., *Adding Insult to Injury: Nancy Fraser Debates Her Critics*. London: Verso. 57–68.

– (2008b). 'Why Overcoming Prejudice Is Not Enough: A Rejoinder to Richard Rorty.' In K. Olson, ed., *Adding Insult to Injury: Nancy Fraser Debates Her Critics*. London: Verso. 82–8.

– (1997). *Justice Interruptus: Critical Reflections on the Postsocialist Condition*. London: Routledge.

Gaetz, S. (2010). 'The Struggle to End Homelessness in Canada: How We Created the Crisis, and How We Can End It.' *Open Health Services and Policy Journal*, 3(1): 21–6.

– (2004). 'Safe Streets for Whom? Homeless Youth, Social Exclusion, and Criminal Victimization.' *Canadian Journal of Criminology and Criminal Justice*, 46(4): 423–55.

Gaetz, S., B. O'Grady, and K. Buccieri. (2010). 'Surviving Crime and Violence: Street Youth and Victimization in Toronto.' A Report for Street Youth Legal Services. www.hsjcc.on.ca (accessed 1 November 2010).

Garland, D. (1996). 'The Limits of the Sovereign State: Strategies of Crime Control in Contemporary Society.' *British Journal of Criminology*, 36(4): 44–67.

Giddens, A. (1994). *Beyond Left and Right: The Future of Radical Politics*. Stanford, Calif.: Stanford University Press.

– (1991). *Modernity and Self-Identity*. Stanford, Calif.: Stanford University Press.

Gilder, G. (1981). *Wealth and Poverty*. New York: Basic Books.

Goodman, L., M. Dutton, and M. Harris. (1997). 'The Relationship between Violence Dimensions and Symptom Severity among Homeless, Mentally Ill Women.' *Journal of Traumatic Stress*, 10(1): 51–70.

– (1995). 'Episodically Homeless Women with Serious Mental Illness: Prevalence of Physical and Sexual Assault.' *American Journal of Orthopsychiatry*, 65(4): 468–78.

Hagan, J., and B. McCarthy. (1997). *Mean Streets: Youth Crime and Homelessness*. New York: Cambridge University Press.

Hagan, J., and C. Albonetti. (1982). 'Race, Class, and the Perception of Criminal Injustice in America.' *American Journal of Sociology*, 88(2): 329–56.

Haggerty, K. (2003). 'From Risk to Precaution: The Rationalities of Personal Crime Prevention.' In R. Ericson and A. Doyle, eds., *Risk and Morality*. Toronto: University of Toronto Press. 193–214.

Harcourt, B. (2001). *Illusion of Order: The False Promise of Broken Windows Policing*. Cambridge, Mass.: Harvard University Press.

Harvey, D. (2011). *The Enigma of Capital and the Crises of Capitalism*. London: Profile Books.

Hatty, S., N. David, and S. Burke. (1999). 'Victimization of Homeless Youth: Public and Private Regimes of Control.' In M. Schwartz and D. Milovanovic, eds., *Race, Gender, and Class in Criminology: The Intersections*. London: Taylor and Francis. 159–91.

Herbert, S. (2006). *Citizens, Cops, and Power: Recognizing the Limits of Community*. Chicago: University of Chicago Press.

– (2001). 'Policing the Contemporary City: Fixing Broken Windows or Shoring up Neo-liberalism?' *Theoretical Criminology*, 5(4): 445–66.

Hiday, V., M. Swartz, J. Swanson, R. Borum, and H. Wagner. (1999). 'Criminal Victimization of Persons with Severe Mental Illness.' *Psychiatric Services*, 50(1): 62–8.

Hobbes, T. (1985 [1651]). *The Leviathan*. London: Penguin.

Hope, T. (2000). 'Inequality and the Clubbing of Private Security.' In T. Hope and R. Sparks, eds., *Crime, Risk and Insecurity*. London: Routledge. 83–106.

Huey, Laura. (2010). 'False Security or Greater Social Inclusion? Exploring Perceptions of CCTV Use in Public and Private Spaces Accessed by the Homeless.' *British Journal of Sociology*, 61(1): 68–86.

– (2009a). 'Homelessness and the "Exclusive Society Thesis": Why It Is Important to "Think Local" to "Act Local" on Homelessness Issues.' *European Journal of Homelessness*, 3: 265–77.

– (2009b). 'The Surveillance Legacy: What Happens to Vancouver's CCTV Systems after the 2010 Olympics?' Security Camera Awareness Network Phase Two Report for the Office of the Privacy Commissioner of Canada. http://www.surveillanceproject.org (accessed 10 September 2010). 66–78.

– (2008). '"When It Comes to Violence in My Place, I Am the Police!" Exploring the Policing Functions of Community Service Providers in Edinburgh's Cowgate and Grassmarket.' *Policing and Society*, 18(3): 207–24.

– (2007). *Negotiating Demands: The Politics of Skid Row Policing in Edinburgh, San Francisco, and Vancouver*. Toronto: University of Toronto Press.

Huey, L., and E. Berndt. (2008). '"You've Gotta Learn How to Play the Game": Homeless Women's Use of Gender Performance as a Tool for Preventing Victimization.' *Sociological Review*, 56(2): 177–94.

Huey, L., K. Walby, and A. Doyle. (2006). 'Cop Watching in the Downtown Eastside: Exploring the Use of (Counter) Surveillance as a Tool of Resistance.' In T. Monahan, ed., *Surveillance and Security: Technological Politics and Power in Everyday Life*. New York: Routledge. 149–65.

Huey, L., and M. Quirouette. (2010a). '"Any Girl Can Call the Cops, No Problem": The Influence of Gender on Support for the Decision to Report Criminal Victimization within Homeless Communities.' *British Journal of Criminology*, 50(2): 278–95.

– (2010b). '"Folks Should Have Access … How You Do It Is the Difficult Thing": Exploring the Importance of Leadership to Maintaining Community Policing Programs for the Homeless.' *Policing and Society*, 20(2): 172–86.

– (2009). 'Access to Justice as a Component of Citizenship: Reconsidering Policing Services for Canada's Homeless.' http://ir.lib.uwo.ca/sociology-pub/10 (accessed 14 September 2010).

Huey, L., and T. Kemple. (2007). '"Let the Streets Take Care of Themselves": Making Historical, Sociological and Common Sense of "Skid Row."' *Urban Studies*, 44(12): 2305–19.

Human Resources and Skills Development Canada (HRSDC). (2011). 'Homelessness Partnering Strategy.' www.hrsdc.gc.ca (accessed 14 May 2011).

Hwang S. (2000). 'Mortality among Men Using Homeless Shelters in Toronto, Ontario.' *Journal of the American Medical Association*, 283: 2152–7.

Jacobs, B., and R. Wright. (2008). 'Moralistic Street Robbery.' *Crime Delinquency*, 54(4): 511–31.

– (2006). *Street Justice: Retaliation in the Criminal Underworld*. Cambridge: Cambridge University Press.

Jasinski, J., J. Wesely, J. Wright, and E. Mustaine. (2010). *Hard Lives, Mean Streets: Violence in the Lives of Homeless Women*. Hanover, Mass.: Northeastern University Press.

Jencks, C. (1992). *Rethinking Social Policy: Race, Poverty, and the Underclass*. Cambridge, Mass.: Harvard University Press.

Johnsen, S., P. Cloke, and J. May. (2005). 'Day Centres for Homeless People: Spaces of Care or Fear?' *Social and Cultural Geography*, 6(6): 787–811.

Johnston, L., and C. Shearing. (2003). *Governing Security*. London: Routledge.

Jones, T., and T. Newburn. (1995). 'How Big Is the Private Security Sector?' *Policing and Society* 5(3): 221–32.

Kennedy, C., and S. Fitzpatrick. (2001). 'Begging, Rough Sleeping and Social Exclusion: Implications for Social Policy.' *Urban Studies*, 38(11): 2001–16.

Kidd, R., and E. Chayet. (1984). 'Why Do Victims Fail to Report? The Psychology of Criminal Victimization.' *Journal of Social Issues*, 41(1): 39–50.

Kipke, M., T. Simon, S. Montgomery, J. Unger, and E. Iversen. (1997). 'Homeless Youth and Their Exposure to and Involvement in Violence While Living on the Streets.' *Journal of Adolescent Health*, 20(3): 360–7.

Knecht, T., and L. Martinez. (2009). 'Humanizing the Homeless: Does Contact Erode Stereotypes?' *Social Science Research*, 38(3): 521–34.

Koegel, P., and M. Burnam. (1987). *The Epidemiology of Alcohol Abuse and Dependence among the Homeless: Findings from the Inner City of Los Angeles*. Rockville, Md.: National Institute on Alcohol Abuse and Alcoholism.

Kushel, M., J. Evans, S. Perry, M. Robertson, and A. Moss. (2003). 'No Door to Lock: Victimization among Homeless and Marginally Housed Persons.' *Archives of Internal Medicine*, 163(10): 2492–9.

Kymlicka, W. 1995. *Multicultural Citizenship*. Oxford: Oxford University Press.

Lam, J., and R. Rosenheck. (1998). 'The Effect of Victimization on Clinical Outcomes of Homeless Persons with Serious Mental Illness.' *Psychiatric Services*, 49(5): 678–683.

Laub, H. (1997). 'Patterns of Criminal Victimization in the United States.' In E. Davis, B. Lee, and C. Schreck. (2005). 'Danger on the Streets: Marginality and Victimization among Homeless People.' *American Behavioral Scientist*, 48(8): 1055–81.

Lister, R. (1998). 'Citizenship on the Margins: Citizenship, Social Work and Social Action.' *European Journal of Social Work*, 1(1): 5–18.

Loader, I. (1999). 'Consumer Culture and the Commodification of Policing and Security.' *Sociology*, 33(2): 373–92.

Loader, I. and N. Walker. (2007). *Civilizing Security*. Cambridge: Cambridge University Press.

– (2006). 'Necessary Virtues: The Legitimate Place of the State in the Production of Security.' In B. Dupont and J. Wood, eds., *Democracy, Society and the Governance of Security*. Cambridge: Cambridge University Press. 165–95.

– (2001). 'Policing as a Public Good: Reconstituting the Connections between Policing and the State.' *Theoretical Criminology*, 5(1): 9–35.

Lurigio, A., and W. Skogan, eds. (1997). *Victims of Crime*, 2nd ed. London: Sage. 9–26.

Lyon, D. (1992). 'The New Surveillance: Electronic Technologies and the Maximum Security Society.' *Crime, Law and Social Change*, 18(1–2): 159–75.

McCarthy, B., J. Hagan, and M. Martin. (2002). 'In and out of Harm's Way: Violent Victimization and the Social Capital of Fictive Street Families.' *Criminology*, 40(4): 831–65.

McCreary Centre Society. (2001). *No Place to Call Home: A Profile of Street Youth in British Columbia*. A report of the McCreary Centre Society.

McIntyre, S. (2005). *Under the Radar: The Sexual Exploitation of Young Men*. www.child.alberta.ca. (accessed 1 November 2010).

Maher, L., E. Dunlap, B. Johnson, and A. Hamid. (1996). 'Gender, Power, and Alternative Living Arrangements in the Inner-City Crack Culture.' *Journal of Research in Crime and Delinquency*, 33(2): 181–205.

Maher, L., and K. Daly. (1997). 'Women in the Street-Level Drug Economy: Continuity or Change?' *Criminology*, 34(4): 465–92.

Marshall, T. (2009 [1950]). 'Citizenship and Social Class.' In J. Manza and M. Sauder, eds., *Inequality and Society*. New York: W.W. Norton. 148–54.

Marsland, D. (1996). *Welfare or Welfare State? Contradictions and Dilemmas in Social Policy*. Houndmills, U.K.: Macmillan.

Mayock, P., and E. O'Sullivan. (2007). *Lives in Crisis: Homeless Young People in Dublin*. Dublin: Liffey Press.

Morphy, L. (2011). 'This Housing Benefit Cut Would Push Many out of Their Homes – to Where?' *The Guardian* (U.K.), http://www.guardian.co.uk (accessed 17 March 2011).

Murray, C. (1999). 'And Now for the Bad News.' *Society*, 37(1): 12–16.

– (1984). *Losing Ground: American Social Policy 1950–1980*. New York: Basic Books.

National Alliance to End Homelessness. (2011). 'State of Homelessness in America,' http://www.naeh.com (accessed 1 June 2011).

Neocleous, M. (2008). *Critique of Security*. Montreal and Kingston, Ont.: McGill-Queen's University Press.

- (2006). 'Theoretical Foundations of the "New Police Science."' In M. Dubber and M. Valverde, eds., *The New Police Science: The Police Power in Domestic and International Governance*. Stanford, Calif.: Stanford University Press. 17–41.

North, C., E. Smith, and E. Spitznagel. (1994). 'Violence and the Homeless: An Epidemiologic Study of Victimization and Aggression.' *Journal of Traumatic Stress*, 7(1): 95–110.

Novac, S., J. Hermer, E. Paradis, and A. Kellen. (2007). 'More Sinned against than Sinning? Homeless People as Victims of Crime and Harassment.' *Centre for Urban and Community Studies Research Bulletin*, 37.

Nyamathi A., B. Leake, and L. Gelberg. (2000). 'Sheltered versus Nonsheltered Homeless Women: Differences in Health, Behavior, Victimization, and Utilization of Care.' *Journal of General Internal Medicine*, 15(5): 565–72.

O'Grady, B., and R. Bright. (2002). 'Squeezed to the Point of Exclusion: The Case of Toronto Squeegee Cleaners.' In Joe Hermer and Janet Mosher, eds., *Disorderly People: Law and the Politics of Exclusion in Ontario*. Halifax, N.S.: Fernwood. 23–39.

O'Malley, P. (2004). 'Globalising Risk? Distinguishing Styles of "Neoliberal" Criminal Justice in Australia and the USA.' In T. Newburn and R. Sparks, eds., *Criminal* Justice and Political Cultures: National and International Dimensions of Crime *Control*. Portland, Ore.: Willan. 30–48.

- (1992). 'Risk, Power and Crime Prevention.' *Economy and Society*, 21(3): 252–75.

O'Malley, P., and D. Palmer. (1996). 'Post-Keynesian Policing.' *Economy and Society*, 25(2): 137–55.

Padgett, D., and E. Streuning. (1992). 'Victimization and Traumatic Injuries among the Homeless: Associations with Alcohol, Drug, and Mental Problems.' *American Journal of Orthopsychiatry*, 62(4): 525–34.

Padgett, D., R. Hawkins, C. Abrams, and A. Davis. (2006). 'In Their Own Words: Trauma and Substance Abuse in the Lives of Formerly Homeless Women with Serious Mental Illness.' *American Journal of Orthopsychiatry*, 76(4): 461–7.

Pain, R., and P. Francis. (2004). 'Living with Crime: Spaces of Risk for Homeless Young People.' *Children's Geographies*, 2(1): 95–110.

Paradise, M., and A. Cauce. (2002). 'Home Street Home: The Interpersonal Dimensions of Adolescent Homelessness.' *Analyses of Social Issues and Public Policy*, 2(1): 223–38.

Parenti, C. (1999). *Lockdown America: Police and Prisons in the Age of Crisis*. London: Verso.

Perron, B., B. Alexander-Eitzman, D. Gillespie, and D. Pollio. (2008). 'Modeling the Mental Health Effects of Victimization among Homeless Persons.' *Social Science and Medicine*, 67(14): 1475–9.

Phelan, J., B. Link, R. Moore, and A. Stueve. (1997). 'The Stigma of
    Homelessness: The Impact of the Label "Homeless" on Attitudes toward
    Poor Persons.' *Social Psychology Quarterly*, 60(4): 323–37.
Phillips, A. (2008). 'From Inequality to Difference: A Severe Case of
    Displacement.' In K. Olson, ed., *Adding Insult to Injury: Nancy Fraser
    Debates Her Critics*. London: Verso. 112–25.
Pyszczynski, T. (2004). 'What Are We So Afraid Of? A Terror Management
    Theory Perspective on the Politics of Fear.' *Social Research*, 71(4): 827–48.
Radley, A., D. Hodgetts, and A. Cullen. (2006). 'Fear, Romance and Transience
    in the Lives of Homeless Women.' *Social and Cultural Geography*, 7(3): 437–61.
Ravenhill, M. (2008). *The Culture of Homelessness*. London: Ashgate.
Reiner, R. (2010). 'Citizenship, Crime, Criminalization: Marshalling a Social
    Democratic Perspective.' *New Criminal Law Review*, 13(2): 241–61.
Reiss, A. (1971). *The Police and the Public*. New Haven, Conn.: Yale University
    Press.
Rigakos, G. (2002). *The New Parapolice: Risk Markets and Commodified Social
    Control*. Toronto: University of Toronto Press.
Roche, B., A. Neaigus, and M. Miller. (2005). 'Street Smarts and Urban Myths:
    Women, Sex Work, and the Role of Storytelling in Risk Reduction and
    Rationalization.' *Medical Anthropology Quarterly*, 19(2): 149–70.
Roebuck, B. (2008). 'Homelessness, Victimization and Crime: Knowledge and
    Actionable Recommendations.' *Report of the Institute for the Prevention of
    Crime*. http://www.prevention-crime.ca (accessed 12 March 2009).
Rose, N. (1999). *Powers of Freedom: Reframing Political Thought*. Cambridge:
    Polity.
– (1996). 'The Death of the Social? Re-Figuring the Territory of Government.'
    Economy and Society, 25(3): 327–56.
Rosenfeld, R., B. Jacobs, and R. Wright. (2003). 'Snitching and the Code of the
    Street.' *British Journal of Criminology*, 43(2): 291–309.
Rossi, P. (1989). *Down and out in America: The Origins of Homelessness*. Chicago:
    University of Chicago Press.
Rousseau, J-J. (1939 [1762]). *The Social Contract or Principles of Political Right*.
    Raleigh, N.C.: Hayes Barton Press.
Roy, E., J. Boivin, N. Haley, and N. Lemire. (1998). 'Mortality among Street
    Youth.' *Lancet*, 352: 32.
Roy, E., N. Haley, P. Leclere, B. Sochanski, J. Boudreau, and J. Boivin. (2004).
    'Mortality in a Cohort of Street Youth in Montreal.' *Journal of the American
    Medical Association*, 292: 569–74.
Rubenstein. K. (2000). 'Citizenship and the Centenary – Inclusion and
    Exclusion in 20th Century Australia.' *Melbourne University Law Review*, 24:
    576–608.

Sandel, M. (1998). *Liberalism and the Limits of Justice*, 2nd ed. Cambridge: Cambridge University Press.

Sanders, T. (2005). 'Rise of the Rent-a-Cop: Private Security in Canada, 1991–2001.' *Canadian Journal of Criminology and Criminal Justice*, 47(1): 175–94.

Saunders, R. (1999). 'The Politics and Practice of Community Policing in Boston.' *Urban Geography*, 20(5): 461–82.

Shannon, K., T. Kerr, S. Allinott, J. Chettiar, J. Shoveller, and M. Tyndall. (2008). 'Social and Structural Violence and Power Relations in Mitigating HIV Risk of Drug-Using Women in Survival Sex Work.' *Social Science and Medicine*, 66: 911–21.

Shearing, C., and P. Stenning. (1984). 'From the Panopticon to Disney World: The Development of Discipline.' In A. Doob and E. Greenspan, eds., *Perspectives in Criminal Law*. Aurora, Ont.: Canada Law Book. 335–49.

Shearing, C., and R. Ericson. (1991). 'Culture as Figurative Action.' *British Journal of Sociology*, 42(4): 481–506.

Shklar, J. (1991). *American Citizenship: The Quest for Inclusion*. Cambridge, Mass.: Harvard University Press.

Simon, J. (2007). *Governing through Crime: How the War on Crime Transformed American Democracy and Created a Culture of Fear*. Oxford: Oxford University Press.

– (2001). 'Entitlement to Cruelty: Neo-Liberalism and the Punitive Mentality in the United States.' In K. Stenson and R. Sullivan, eds., *Crime, Risk and Justice: The Politics of Crime Control in Liberal Democracies*. Portland, Ore.: Willan. 125–43.

Simons, R., and L. Whitbeck. (1991). 'Sexual Abuse as a Precursor to Prostitution and Victimization among Adolescent and Adult Homeless Women.' *Journal of Family*, 12(3): 361–80.

Singer, S. (1988). 'The Fear of Reprisal and the Failure of Victims to Report a Personal Crime.' *Journal of Quantitative Criminology*, 4(3): 289–302.

Singh, A-M. (2005). 'Private Security and Crime Control.' *Theoretical Criminology*, 9(2): 153–74.

Skogan, W. (1984). 'Reporting Crimes to the Police: The Status of World Research.' *Journal of Research in Crime and Delinquency*, 21(1): 113–37.

– (1976). 'Citizens Reporting of Crime: Some National Panel Data.' *Criminology*, 13(4): 535–49.

Spitzer, S. (1975). 'Toward a Marxist Theory of Deviance.' *Social Problems*, 22: 638–51.

Spitzer, S., and A. Scull. (1992). 'Privatization and Capitalist Development: The Case of the Private Police.' In K. McCormick and L. Visano, eds., *Understanding Policing*. Toronto: Canadian Scholars' Press. 57–82.

Stenson, K. (2001). 'The New Politics of Crime Control.' In K. Stenson and R. Sullivan, eds., *Crime, Risk and Justice: The Politics of Crime Control in Liberal Democracies*. Portland, Ore.: Willan. 15–28.

– (1993). 'Community Policing as a Governmental Technology.' *Economy and Society*, 22(3): 373–89.

Stenson, K., and A. Edwards. (2001). 'Re-Thinking Crime Control in Advanced Liberal Government: The "Third Way" and the Return to the Local.' In K. Stenson and R. Sullivan, eds., *Crime, Risk and Justice: The Politics of Crime Control in Liberal Democracies*. Portland, Ore.: Willan. 68–86.

Stermac, L., and E. Paradis. (2001). 'Homeless Women and Victimization: Abuse and Mental Health History among Homeless Rape Survivors.' *Resources for Feminist Research*, 28(3/4): 65–75.

Sullivan, G., A. Burnam, P. Koegel, and J. Hollenberg. (2000). 'Quality of Life of Homeless Persons with Mental Illness: Results from the Course-of-Homelessness Study.' *Psychiatric Services*, 51(9): 1135–41.

Sullivan, R. (2001). 'The Schizophrenic State: Neo-Liberal Criminal Justice.' In K. Stenson and R. Sullivan, eds., *Crime, Risk and Justice: The Politics of Crime Control in Liberal Democracies*. Portland, Ore.: Willan. 29–48.

Tarling, R., and K. Morris. (2010). 'Reporting Crime to the Police.' *British Journal of Criminology*, 50(2): 474–90.

Thompson, L. (2010). 'Statutory Homelessness: September Quarter 2010 England.' http://www.communities.gov.uk (accessed 23 May 2011).

Tonry, M. (2004). *Thinking about Crime: Sense and Sensibility in American Penal Culture*. New York: Oxford University Press.

Tucker, J., S. Wenzel, J. Straus, G. Ryan, and D. Golinelli. (2005). 'Experiencing Interpersonal Violence: Perspectives of Sexually Active, Substance-Using Women Living in Shelters and Low-Income Housing.' *Violence against Women*, 11(10): 1319–40.

Turner, B. (2009), 'T.H. Marshall, Social Rights and English National Identity.' *Citizenship Studies*, 13(1): 65–73.

Tyler, K. (2008). 'A Comparison of Risk Factors for Sexual Victimization among Gay, Lesbian, Bisexual, and Heterosexual Homeless Young Adults.' *Violence and Victims*, 23(5): 586–602.

Tyler, K., and K. Johnson. (2004). 'Victims and Offenders: Accounts of Paybacks, Invulnerability, and Financial Gain among Homeless Youth.' *Deviant Behavior*, 25(5): 427–49.

Tyler, K., L. Whitbeck, and A. Cauce. (2001). 'The Impact of Childhood Sexual Abuse on Later Sexual Victimization among Runaway Youth.' *Journal of Research on Adolescence*, 11(1): 151–76.

Tyler, K., L. Whitbeck, D. Hoyt, and A. Cauce. (2004). 'Risk Factors for Sexual Victimization among Male and Female Homeless and Runaway Youth.' *Journal of Interpersonal Violence*, 19(5): 503–20.

U.K. Office for National Statistics. (2011). 'Unemployment Rate.' http://www.statistics.gov.uk (accessed 23 May 2011).

Valverde, M. (2001). 'Governing Security, Governing through Security.' In R. Daniels, P. Mackem, and K. Roach, eds., *The Security of Freedom: Essays on Canada's Anti-Terrorism Bill*. Toronto: University of Toronto Press.

Vance, D. (1995). 'A Portrait of Older Homeless Men: Identifying Hopelessness and Adaptation.' *Journal of Social Distress and the Homeless*, 4(1): 57–71.

Wachholz, S. (2005). 'Hate Crimes against the Homeless: Warning-Out New England Style.' *Journal of Sociology and Social Welfare*, 32(4): 141–63.

Wallace, D., N. Hirschinger-Blank, and J. Grisso. (2008). 'Female-Female Non-Partner Assault: A Political-Economic Theory of Street Inner City Codes and Female-Gendered Culture in the Contemporary African-American Inner City.' *Critical Sociology*, 34(2): 271–90.

Wardhaugh, J. (2000). *Sub City: Young People, Homelessness and Crime*. Aldershot, U.K.: Ashgate.

WeTip. (2010). http://www.wetip.com (accessed 4 June 2010).

Weber, C. (2008). 'Designing Safe Citizens.' *Citizenship Studies*, 12(2): 125–42.

Wenzel, S., B. Leake, and L. Gelberg. (2001). 'Risk Factors for Major Violence among Homeless Women.' *Journal of Interpersonal Violence*, 16(8): 739–52.

Wesely, J., and J. Wright. (2009). 'From the Inside Out: Efforts by Homeless Women to Disrupt Cycles of Crime and Violence.' *Women and Criminal Justice*, 19(3): 217–34.

Whitbeck, L., and D. Hoyt. (1999). *Nowhere to Grow*. New York: Walter de Gruyter.

Whitbeck, L., D. Hoyt, and D. and K. Ackley. (1997). 'Abusive Family Backgrounds and Later Victimization among Runaway and Homeless Adolescents.' *Journal of Research on Adolescence*, 7(3): 375–92.

Whitbeck, L., D. Hoyt, and K. Yoder. (1999). 'A Risk-Amplification Model of Victimization and Depressive Symptoms among Runaway and Homeless Adolescents.' *American Journal of Community Psychology*, 27(2): 273–96.

Whitbeck, L., D. Hoyt, K. Yoder, A. Cauce, and M. Paradise. (2001). 'Deviant Behavior and Victimization among Homeless and Runaway Adolescents.' *Journal of Interpersonal Violence*, 16(11): 1175–1204.

Whitbeck, L., and R. Simons. (1990). 'Life on the Streets: The Victimization of Runaway and Homeless Adolescents.' *Youth and Society*, 22(1): 108–25.

Whitzman, C. (2006). 'At the Intersection of Invisibilities: Canadian Women, Homelessness and Health outside the "Big City." *Gender, Place and Culture,* 13(4): 383–99.

Wilson, W. (1987). *The Truly Disadvantaged: The Inner City, the Underclass and Public Policy.* Chicago: University of Chicago Press.

Wingert, S., N. Higgitt, and J. Ristock. (2005). 'Voices from the Margins: Understanding Street Youth in Winnipeg.' *Canadian Journal of Urban Research,* 14(1): 54–80.

Wood, J., and K. Edwards. (2005). 'Victimization of Mentally Ill Patients Living in the Community: Is It a Lifestyle Issue?' *Legal and Criminological Psychology,* 10(2): 279–90.

Wright, J. (2009 [1989]). *Address Unknown: The Homeless in America.* New York: Transaction.

Yates, J. (2000). '"You Just Don't Grass": Youth, Crime and Grassing in a Working Class Community.' *Youth Justice,* 6(3): 195–210.

Young, J. (1999). *The Exclusive Society.* London: Sage.

Zedner, L. (2009). *Security.* London: Routledge.

– (2003). 'Too Much Security?' *International Journal of the Sociology of Law,* 31(1): 155–84.

Index